D0408278

SHAME

SHAME

How America's Past Sins
Have Polarized Our Country

—◦((●))◦—

SHELBY STEELE

BASIC BOOKS

A Member of the Perseus Books Group
New York

Copyright © 2015 by Shelby Steele

Published by Basic Books,

A Member of the Perseus Books Group

All rights reserved. Printed in the United States of America. No part of this
book may be reproduced in any manner whatsoever without written permis-
sion except in the case of brief quotations embodied in critical articles and
reviews. For information, address Basic Books, 250 West 57th Street,
New York, NY 10107.

Books published by Basic Books are available at special discounts for bulk
purchases in the United States by corporations, institutions, and other
organizations. For more information, please contact the Special Markets
Department at the Perseus Books Group, 2300 Chestnut Street, Suite 200,
Philadelphia, PA 19103, or call (800) 810-4145, ext. 5000, or e-mail
special.markets@perseusbooks.com.

Designed by Pauline Brown

Library of Congress Cataloging-in-Publication Data

Steele, Shelby.
    Shame : how America's past sins have polarized our country / Shelby Steele.
        pages cm
    Includes index.
    ISBN 978-0-465-06697-1 (hardback) — ISBN 978-0-465-04055-1
(e-book) 1. United States—Race relations. 2. Equality—United States.
3. Discrimination—United States. 4. Minorities—United States—
Social conditions. 5. United States—Social policy. 6. United States—
Politics and government. I. Title.
    E184.A1.S767 2015
    305.800973—dc23

                                                        2014046421

10 9 8 7 6 5 4 3 2 1

I would like to dedicate this book to my wife, Rita Steele, whose criticisms and labors have made it a better book.

CONTENTS

1

The Great Divide

NOT LONG AGO I was the lone conservative at a panel discussion on race and politics at the famous Aspen Institute in Colorado. The day before the panel was to take place, some of us were asked—as a way of opening what was to be a weeklong conference—to say a few words about what we wanted most for America. This was surely a summons to grandiosity, but it did trigger a thought. When my turn came I said that what I wanted most for America was an end to white guilt, or at least an ebbing of this guilt into insignificance. I then used my allotted few minutes to define white guilt as the terror of being seen as racist—a terror that has caused whites to act guiltily toward minorities even when they feel no actual guilt. My point was that this terror—and the lust it has inspired in whites to show themselves innocent of racism—has spawned a new white paternalism toward minorities since the 1960s that, among other things, has damaged the black family more profoundly than segregation ever did.

I also pleaded especially for an end to the condescension of affirmative action, only to realize halfway through my remarks that the slightly slumping woman in the front row was none other than retired Supreme Court justice Sandra Day O'Connor—the justice whose 2003 opinion in *Grutter v. Michigan* has effectively extended the life of affirmative action for another twenty-five years. But it was too late by then to take her feelings into account, so I finished on theme: the benevolent paternalism of white guilt, I said, had injured the self-esteem, if not the souls, of minorities in ways that the malevolent paternalism of white racism never had.

Post-1960s welfare policies, the proliferation of "identity politics" and group preferences, and all the grandiose social interventions of the War on Poverty and the Great Society—all this was meant to redeem the nation from its bigoted past, but paradoxically, it also invited minorities to make an identity and a politics out of grievance and inferiority. Its seductive whisper to them was that their collective grievance was their entitlement and that protest politics was the best way to cash in on that entitlement—this at the precise moment when America was at last beginning to free up minorities as individual citizens who could pursue their own happiness to the limits of their abilities. Thus, white guilt was a smothering and distracting kindness that enmeshed minorities more in the struggle for white redemption than in their own struggle to develop as individuals capable of competing with all others.

Of course, this was a mouthful, and something close to sacrilege at the liberal-leaning Aspen Institute. I had set out only to say what I truly meant, not to be provocative or to discomfit a retired Supreme Court justice. Yet I had been provocative all the same, and I may have also discomfited Justice O'Connor—not because I intended either outcome, but simply because I had offered up what was considered to be a "conservative" analysis of race in America.

The real provocation was in the very *idea* of looking at race in America through a lens of "classic" Jeffersonian liberalism—that liberalism which sought freedom for the individual above all else. This was the liberalism that had actually given us the civil rights movement of the 1950s and early 1960s. In that era, Martin Luther King Jr. was already recognizable as an American archetype precisely because he was so aligned with the central principle of this liberalism: individual freedom. I wanted to celebrate this liberalism and argue that a free society—not necessarily free of all bigotry, but certainly free of all illegal discrimination—was what

America owed minorities. After that we minorities should simply be left alone. We should not be smothered, as we have been, by the new paternalistic liberalism that emerged in the mid-1960s—a guilt-driven liberalism that has imposed itself through a series of ineffective and even destructive government programs and policies. We should be left to find our own way as free men and women in this fast-paced and highly competitive society.

In many ways the minority struggle for freedom—just like white America's long-ago struggle for freedom from British rule—has been a battle to have no oppressive or capricious power intervene between the individual and his pursuit of happiness. How, then, does it constitute progress for minorities to overcome bigotry as a limit on their freedom only to subjugate themselves to a paternalistic interventionism inspired by white guilt? There is no true freedom either way.

This was the impropriety, the lapse of good manners that made for provocation. A freedom that could not guarantee a positive outcome for blacks (America's classic victims) was perceived as unfair. So whether I was right or wrong was irrelevant next to the unseemliness of speaking about black Americans in the light of self-help and individual responsibility—two entirely conventional values that came to be labeled "conservative" only after the 1960s, and then primarily in relation to minorities.

I am used to being in situations where mention of such "conservative" values amounts to an impropriety. On today's political landscape, there are few people more inherently provocative, more unforeseen and unsettling, than people like myself who are designated "black conservative." All the other permutations of racial and political identity are expected—white liberal or white conservative, Hispanic liberal or Hispanic conservative, black liberal. We know their cultural profiles: the Hispanic who is hard working, Catholic, and conservative; the upscale Connecticut white liberal; the black of almost any background who is presumed liberal simply for being black. Black conservatives confound expectation. Worse, we *seem* to put the moral authority that comes from our race's great suffering into the service of an ideology (conservatism) that many see as a source of that suffering. By this logic, the black conservative can only be opportunistic or, worse, self-hating and sycophantic. So in a setting like the Aspen Institute, where liberalism is simple etiquette and where criticism of minorities is verboten, the black conservative inevitably gives offense.

———————————

AND I SAW THAT MY little "end-of-white-guilt" speech had done just that when I arrived the next day for my panel discussion on race and politics. As I stepped onto the stage,

the moderator of my panel—a solicitous young black writer
who kept reassuring me that he would be fair to me despite
the obvious gulf between us—immediately called me into
a huddle. And there I was confronted with a very agitated
young white man, someone not on the panel, who implored
me to give him a few minutes with the audience before the
panel began so that he could respond to my remarks of
the previous day. It was my call to make, and simple common sense told me to say no. Clearly this was someone who
had spent the previous twenty-four hours stewing in outrage
over my call for an end to white guilt. Why give a platform
to such an openly declared enemy? But then I heard myself
say, "Go right ahead."

He looked startled, and then rushed to the podium as if
afraid that I might change my mind. But I wouldn't have.
I try to follow that ethic by which one gives wide berth
to one's opposition. So I took my designated chair on the
panel and listened as this jumpy young man beseeched
the audience not to believe what I had said the day before.
He was slight and blond, likely a graduate student, and he
spoke with a kind of mimed passion that made him seem
theatrical. For effect, he would occasionally look over his
shoulder at me as if to shudder at an unspeakable menace.
He wanted this nice and unsuspecting Aspen audience to
know that I was selling false consolation by seducing them
into the fiction that white guilt was now a greater problem

for minorities than white racism. He wanted to reassure them that blacks were still suffering in America and that racism, discrimination, and inequality were still alive—still great barriers to black advancement.

My first reaction to people like this young man is always the same: Where were you when I needed you? I had grown up in the rigid segregation of 1950s Chicago, where my life had been entirely circumscribed by white racism. Residential segregation was nearly absolute. My elementary school triggered the first desegregation lawsuit in the North. My family was afraid to cross the threshold of any restaurant until I was almost twenty years old. The only jobs open to me in high school were as a field hand or as a yard boy. My high-school guidance counselor said flatly that manual labor would be my employment horizon. My life had to always be negotiated around my failure to be white. I knew decent white people, but these "good whites"—people who would defy the strictures of segregation—were the exception. Even the Kennedy brothers, Jack and Bobby, came only reluctantly—grudgingly at first, in Bobby's case—to the cause of civil rights.

So there had been a time when blacks needed people like this young man. But on that afternoon in Aspen we were almost fifty years removed from that time, and this young man was only pretending to the heroism of those "good whites" who, back in the civil rights era, had actually

"spoken truth to power"—whites who had risked their ca-
reers, their families, their standing in their communities,
and even their lives. But there was no such risk for this
young man in Aspen, no jeopardy against which he might
show himself heroic. Here he was a redundancy: a man protesting racism to people for whom it was already anathema.

Still, I suspected that most people in that auditorium
broadly agreed with him, even if they thought him a gate-
crasher and a poseur. In fact his appearance had the feel of
a ritual, as if it were somehow an expected and necessary
event. And when I heard the alarm in his voice at what I'd
said the day before, something occurred to me: by coming
to a place like Aspen and saying the things I had said, I
had—so to speak—thrown the conference slightly out
of alignment. The Aspen Conference had a certain idea of
itself, an identity: it wanted quality intellectual dialogue
within a progressive to liberal-centrist political orientation.
My remarks had pushed me off this political continuum
altogether and solidly into conservative territory. After
all, I had implied that post-1960s liberalism was the new
enemy—and not the friend—of minorities at a conference
where conventional wisdom held the opposite to be true.

So, in effect, my young nemesis had spoken out in order
to bring the conference back into alignment, to enforce
the boundaries of the new liberal identity. He wanted this
friendly, upscale, and overwhelmingly white crowd to see

me as a snake in the garden of their liberal identity, enticing them with the "apple" of an escape from white guilt. He wanted them to understand that the price they might pay for listening to someone like me could be much higher than they thought: they could lose their liberal identity itself and, along with it, the good opinion of themselves as decent and socially concerned people. I wasn't just a threat to their politics. I threatened them with a kind of moral disgrace—since their agreement with any part of my argument would open them to charges of racism. Of course, he never said it, but he wanted no serious discussion of ideas or of public policy. Arguing thoughtfully would only make me less a snake, and, above all else, he wanted to mark me as an outsider.

When he finally left the stage and took a seat in the audience, I was invited to respond. But I had no heart for it. He hadn't made a real argument, but had essentially only tried to make me an untouchable—someone from a dark realm of ideas who was at once seductive and evil. To answer him would be to argue with the rhetorical equivalent of an impression, a blur of indistinct ideas—to punch at shadows. Finally the panel moderator moved us into our discussion format. I never saw this young interloper again.

———————

THE FACT IS THAT this young man and I come from two very different Americas. The shorthand for these two Americas might be "liberal" and "conservative," but this would indeed be a shorthand. These labels once signified something much less incendiary than they do today; they were opposing political orientations, but they shared a common national identity. One was conservative or liberal but within a fairly non-contentious cultural understanding of what it meant to be American. But since the 1960s, "liberal" and "conservative" have come to function almost like national identities in their own right. To be one or the other is not merely to lean left or right—toward "labor" or toward "business"— within a common national identity; it is to belong to a different vision of America altogether, a vision that seeks to supersede the opposing vision and to establish itself as the nation's common identity. Today the Left and the Right don't work within a shared understanding of the national purpose; nor do they seek such an understanding. Rather, each seeks to win out over the other and to define the nation by its own terms.

It was all the turmoil of the 1960s—the civil rights and women's movements, Vietnam, the sexual revolution, and so on—that triggered this change by making it clear that America could not go back to being the country it had been before. It would have to reinvent itself. It would have to become a better country. Thus, the reinvention of America as a country shorn of its past sins became an unspoken, though extremely powerful, mandate in our national politics. Liberals and conservatives could no longer think of themselves simply as political rivals competing within a common and settled American identity. That identity was no longer settled—or even legitimate—because it was stigmatized in the 1960s as racist, sexist, and imperialistic. The very legitimacy of our democratic society demanded that America be reimagined in the reverse of this stigmatization.

This sea change meant that American liberals and conservatives were called upon to fill a void, to articulate a new and legitimate American identity. It was no longer enough for the proponents of these perspectives merely to vie over the issues of the day. Both worldviews would now have to evolve into full-blown ideologies capable of projecting a new political and cultural vision of America. Both liberals and conservatives would have to revisit their first principles, seek philosophical coherence between their own view and contemporary events, enlist intellectuals, and engage in ongoing debate. In other words, people on both sides would have to conjure up an America unique to their own first principles and beliefs—an America that epitomized all they longed for. And it fell on both liberals and conservatives to fight for their own America, to demand that it prevail over the opposing vision of the nation—and to provide America with a new singular and unifying identity.

This is how the mandate of the 1960s to reinvent America launched the infamous "culture war" between liberalism and conservatism—a war that we Americans wage to this day with undiminished fervor. After the1960s, the American identity became a self-conscious mission in our politics, so that liberals and conservatives had to contend with each other over identity as well as public policy. When we argue over health care or immigration or Middle East policy, it is as if two distinct Americas were arguing, each with a different idea of what it means to be an American. And these arguments are intense and often uncivil, because each side feels that its American identity is at risk from the other side. So the conflict is very much a culture *war*, with each side longing for "victory" over the other, and each side seeing itself as America's last and best hope.

This makes for a great irony in contemporary American life: although we have come very far in overcoming old sins, such as racism and sexism, we are in many ways more sharply divided than when those sins went largely unchallenged. The culture war drew us into a very polarizing progression in which liberalism and conservatism evolved into broad cultural identities that, in turn, sought to manifest themselves in actual territorial dominance—each hoping to ultimately become the nation's singular identity. Since the 1960s, this war has divided up our culture into what might be called "identity territories." America's universities are now almost exclusively left-leaning; most public-policy think tanks are right-leaning. Talk radio is conservative; National Public Radio and the major television networks are liberal. On cable television, almost every news and commentary channel is a recognizable identity territory—Fox/right; MSNBC/left; CNN/left. In the print media our two great national newspapers are the liberal *New York Times* and the conservative *Wall Street Journal* (especially in the editorial pages). The Pulitzer Prize and MacArthur Grants are left; the Bradley Prize is right. The blogosphere is notoriously divided by political stripe. And then there are "red" and "blue" states, cities, towns, and even neighborhoods. At election time, Americans can see on television a graphic of their culture war: those blue and red electoral maps that give us a virtual topography of political identity.

———————

TODAY, A LIBERAL OR A CONSERVATIVE can proudly identify with the image of America projected by their chosen ideology in the same way that most Americans in the 1950s proudly identified with a victorious and prosperous postwar America. In the America envisioned by both ideologies, there is no racism or sexism or imperialism to be embarrassed by. After all, ideologies project idealized images of the near-perfect America that they promise to deliver. Thus, in one's ideological identity, one can find the innocence that is no longer possible—since the 1960s—in America's defamed national identity.

To announce oneself as a liberal or a conservative is like announcing oneself as a Frenchman or a Brit. It is virtually an announcement of tribal identity, and it means something much larger than ideology. To be a Brit is a God-given fate that is likely to stir far deeper passions than everyday political debates. Nationalism—the nationalist impulse—is passion itself; it is atavistic, beyond the reach of reason, a secular sacredness. The nationalist is expected to be intolerant of all opposition to his nation's sovereignty, and is most often willing to defend that sovereignty with his life.

Well, when we let nationalism shape the form of our liberal or conservative identities—when we practice our ideological leaning as if it were a divine right, an atavism to be defended at all cost—then we put ourselves on a warlike footing. We feel an impunity toward our opposition, and we grant ourselves a scorched-earth license to fight back. They are not the other side of the same coin; they are a different coin altogether, a fundamentally illegitimate and alien force. And we are forgiven our bitterness and contempt for them.

———————

THIS WAS THE CONTEMPT that the young man at Aspen had flashed my way. He had crashed the event to defend a sovereignty, and he had felt the license to disrupt. Liberalism was his nationality, and who compromises their nationality? He had spoken from his commandeered podium like a patriot.

But, then, I had to wonder if my own ideological orientation had somehow taken the form of nationalistic fervor. Was I a blind patriot rather than a thinking man? Was my loyalty to conservatism grounded in experience and thought, or in blood fealty to an ideology that sees itself as a sovereign nation? For me, conservatism revolves around the principles and the disciplines of freedom, and through its lens I can see the America that I have always wanted. So, yes, like my young nemesis, I could experience my ideology as a nationalism. But unlike him I wanted to discipline that impulse, to subject my ideology—and all the policies it fostered—to every sort of test of truth and effectiveness. And I was ready to modify accordingly, to disabuse myself of even long-held beliefs that didn't pan out in reality. It was exactly this loyalty to fact over ideology that had driven me away from liberalism in the 1970s and 1980s into an appreciation of conservatism's commitment to individual freedom. In other words, for me, ideology does not precede truth. Rather, truth, as best as we can know it, is always the test of ideology. I want my fervor for conservatism to be disciplined by a deep and abiding humility. Passion is one thing, but "true belief" is blindness.

——————————

FOR THE YOUNG MAN IN ASPEN, ideological identity clearly
preceded truth. He represents for me a very specific fallacy
that might be called "poetic truth." Poetic license occurs
when poets take a certain liberty with the conventional rules
of grammar and syntax in order to achieve an effect. They
break the rules in order to create a more beautiful or more
powerful effect than would otherwise be possible. Adapting
this idea of license and rule breaking to the realm of ideology, we might say that "poetic truth" disregards the actual
truth in order to assert a larger *essential* truth that supports
one's ideological position. It makes the actual truth seem
secondary or irrelevant. Poetic truths defend the sovereignty
of one's ideological identity by taking license with reality
and fact. They work by moral intimidation rather than by
reason, so that even to question them is heresy.

The young man's poetic truth was that the victimization of blacks (and other minorities) is *always* the larger
truth of American life, a truth so much a part of America's fundamental character that it must always be taken
as literal truth even when the facts refute it. When poetic
truth is in play, facts carry no weight. For him the essential
truth—the truth for which he demanded moral and political accountability—was that America was an intractably

racist society, maybe a little better today than in the past, but still structurally aligned against blacks and minorities. In my little end-of-white-guilt speech I had stated a hard fact: that since the 1960s, white racism had lost so much of its authority, power, and legitimacy that it was no longer, in itself, a prohibitive barrier to black advancement. Blacks have now risen to every level of American society, including the presidency. If you are black and you want to be a poet, or a doctor, or a corporate executive, or a movie star, there will surely be barriers to overcome, but white racism will be among the least of them. You will be far more likely to receive racial preferences than to suffer racial discrimination.

Those who doubt this will always point to today's long litany of racial disparities. Blacks are still behind virtually all other groups by the most important measures of social and economic well-being: educational achievement, home ownership, employment levels, academic test scores, marriage rates, household net worth, and so on. The fact that seven out of ten black women are single, along with the fact that 70 percent of first black marriages fail (47 percent for whites), means that black women are married at roughly half the rate of white women and divorced at twice the rate. Thus it is not surprising that nearly three-quarters of all black children are born out of wedlock.

In 2008, black college students were three times more likely than whites to graduate with a grade point average below a meager 2.5—this on top of a graduation rate for blacks of only 42 percent, according to the *Journal of Blacks in Higher Education*. Consequently, blacks in general have the highest college dropout rate and the lowest grade point average of any student group in America, with the arguable exception of reservation Indians. And, yes, these disparities— and many others—most certainly had their genesis in centuries of racial oppression. But post-1960s liberalism conflates the past with the present: it argues that today's racial disparities are caused by precisely the same white racism that caused them in the past—thus the poetic truth that blacks today remain stymied and victimized by white racism.

But past oppression cannot be conflated into present-day oppression. It is likely, for example, that today's racial disparities are due more to dysfunctions within the black community, and—I would argue—to liberal social policies that have encouraged us to trade more on our past victimization than to overcome the damage done by that victimization through dint of our own pride and will. One can say this stance "blames the victim" by making him responsible for the injury done him by bigotry and oppression. But there also comes a time when he must stop thinking of himself as a victim by acknowledging that—existentially—his fate is always in his own hands. One of the more pernicious corruptions of post-1960s liberalism is that it undermined the spirit of self-help and individual responsibility in precisely the people it sought to uplift.

Segregation, for all its obvious evil, at least left our fate in our own hands, which is why we—in the face of more government opposition than assistance—generated one of the most effective and articulate movements for human freedom the world has ever seen. Without any government grants, and in a society that ran the gamut from cool indifference toward us to murderous terrorism against us, we expanded the American democracy beyond the color line.

But all this was not relevant to the young man in Aspen, because it was subversive of his "poetic" commitment to black victimization—and therefore to his ideological identity. So the truth—that blacks had now achieved a level of freedom comparable to that of all others—was cast as a dangerous lie. He beseeched the good people in the audience not to be confused or seduced by this actual fact—and above all else not to allow their politics to follow from such a fact. He wanted them to feel that if they accepted what was so obviously true, they would be aligning themselves with America's terrible history of racism. Only by supporting what was not true—that racism was still the greatest barrier to black advancement—could they prove themselves innocent of racism.

Poetic truth—this assertion of a broad characteristic "truth" that invalidates actual truth—is contemporary liberalism's greatest source of power. It is also liberalism's most fundamental corruption.

————————

WHY WOULD PEOPLE ALLOW themselves to be manipulated into disregarding self-evident truth in favor of some sweeping and largely unsupportable claim of truth? Because, I think, the great trick of modern liberalism is to link its poetic truths (false as they may be) with innocence from all the great sins of America's past—racism, sexism, imperialism, capitalist greed, and so on—and, similarly, to stain the actual truth with those selfsame sins. So, if you want to be politically correct, if you want to be seen as someone who is cleansed of America's past ugliness, you will go along with the poetic truth that racism is still a great barrier for blacks. Conversely, embracing the literal truth—that racism is no longer a serious barrier—will make you politically incorrect and will stigmatize you with that ugliness.

But poetic truth is not about truth; it's about power. It is a formula for power. Historically, freedom was always the great imperative of liberalism; poetic truth enabled liberals after the 1960s to shift that imperative from freedom to morality. A distinction must be made. During and immediately after the 1960s, racism and sexism were still more literal truth than poetic truth. As we moved through the 1970s,

1980s, and 1990s, America morally evolved so that these old American evils became more "poetic" than literal. Yet redeeming America from these evils has become liberalism's rationale for demanding real power in the real world—the political and cultural power to create social programs, to socially engineer on a national scale, to expand welfare, to entrench group preferences in American institutions, and so on. But what happens to liberal power when America actually earns considerable redemption—when there are more women than men in the nation's medical schools, when a black can serve as the president, when public accommodations are open to anyone with the price of the ticket?

What actually happened was that liberalism turned to poetic truth when America's past sins were no longer literally true enough to support liberal policies and the liberal claim on power. The poetic truth of black victimization seeks to compensate for America's moral evolution. It tries to keep alive the justification for liberal power even as that justification has been greatly nullified by America's moral development. The poetic idea that America will always be a racist, sexist, imperialistic, and greed-driven society has rescued post-1960s liberalism from the great diminishment that should have been its fate, given the literal truth of America's remarkable (if incomplete) moral growth.

My young antagonist in Aspen was not agitated by some racial injustice. He would have only relished a bit of good old-fashioned racial injustice, since it would have justified his entire political identity. He was agitated by the implication that white America had morally evolved. It wasn't America's old evils that bothered him; he was afraid of America's moral growth. That growth threatened him with obsolescence and irrelevancy. It threatened to turn him into an embarrassment.

BUT WHY IS THE "GREAT DIVIDE" between this young man and myself—and, far more importantly, between liberal and conservative America—such an urgent problem for America today? One reason may be that a divide like this suggests that America has in fact become two Americas, two political cultures forever locked in a "cold war" within a single society. This implies a spiritual schism within America itself, and, following from that, the prospect of perpetual and hopeless debate—the kind of ego-driven debate in which both sides want the other side to "think like us." There is a little of what Sigmund Freud called the "narcissism of small difference" in all this. Neighboring nations often have a far greater animus toward each other than they do toward distant nations that are more starkly opposed to their interests and values. Today, liberal and conservative Americans are often contemptuous of each other with a passion that would more logically be reserved for foreign enemies.

But the urgency of this "great divide" also has a less obvious explanation. Our national debate over foreign and domestic issues has come to be framed as much by poetic truths as by dispassionate assessments of the realities we face. Again, the poetic truth that blacks are still held back from full equality by ongoing "structural" racism carries more authority than the objective truth: that today racism is not remotely the barrier to black advancement in American life that it once was. In foreign affairs, the poetic truth that we Americans are essentially imperialistic cowboys bent on exploiting the world has more credibility than the obvious truth, which is that our wealth and power (accumulated over centuries of unprecedented innovation in a context of freedom) has often drawn us into the unwanted role of policing a turbulent world—and, it must be added, to the world's immense benefit.

The great problem with poetic truths is that they are never self-evident in the way, for example, that racial victimization was self-evident in the era of segregation. Today the actual facts fail to support the notion that racial victimization is a prevailing truth of American life. So today, a poetic truth, like "black victimization," or the ongoing "repression of women," or the systematic "abuse of the environment," must be imposed on society not by fact and reason but by some regime of political correctness—some notion of propriety and decency that coerces people into treating such claims as actual fact. If you don't presume that America's racism, sexism, warmongering, and environmental disregard are incontrovertible qualities of the American character, then you are obviously "incorrect" and guilty of fellow traveling with precisely those qualities.

Political correctness is the enforcement arm of poetic truth. It coerces people into suspending their own judgment on matters of racial equality, women's rights, war, and the environment in deference to some prescribed "correct" view on these matters that will distance them from the stigma of America's sinful past. The very point of poetic truths is to supplant the actual reality of American life with the view of America as a nation still surreptitiously devoted to its past sins. It has no other purpose than to project these sins as the essential, if not the eternal, truth of the American way of life. Then political correctness tries to bully and shame Americans—on pain of their human decency—into conformity with this ugly view of their society.

This is how America after the 1960s began to live under a hegemony of political correctness, so that we became more invested in the prescriptions of that correctness than in the true nature of the problems we faced.

The young man at Aspen demanded to speak so that he could corral people back into a prescribed correctness and away from a more open-minded approach to the complex problems that our racial history has left us to deal with—

problems that the former victims of this history will certainly bear the greatest responsibility for overcoming. The prescriptions of political correctness offered him a glib innocence of all this. He could subscribe to "diversity," "inclusiveness," and "social justice" and think himself solidly on the side of the good. The problem is that these prescriptions only throw fuzzy and unattainable idealisms at profound problems— problems rooted in the long centuries of dehumanization visited on minorities and women. What is "diversity" beyond a vague apologia, an amorphous expression of goodwill that offers no objective assessment whatsoever of the actual problems that minority groups face?

The point is that those poetic truths, and the notions of correctness that force them on society, prevent America from seeing itself accurately. That is their purpose. They pull down the curtain on what is actually true. If decades of government assistance have weakened the black family with dependency and dysfunction, poetic truth argues all the more fervently that blacks are victims and that whites are privileged. Poetic truths stigmatize the actual truth with the sins of America's past so that truth itself becomes "incorrect."

As America has become more "correct" in relation to its past, it has also become more cut off from the reality of its present. The danger here is that the nation's innocence— its redemption from past sins—becomes linked to a kind of know-nothingism. We can't afford to know, for example, that America's military might—a vulgarity in the minds of many—has stabilized vast stretches of Asia and Europe since World War II, so that nations under the umbrella of our power have become prosperous trading partners today. We can't admit today that the lives of minorities are no longer stunted by either prejudice or "white privilege." And we can't afford to acknowledge that the same is true for American women. Contrition and apology are "correct"; honesty is "incorrect."

In this way, today's great liberal-conservative divide puts correctness at odds with the kind of forthright self-examination that societies need to do in order to understand the true nature of the problems they face. Frank self-examination puts one at risk of transgressing correctness. So issues like free markets versus redistributive economics, educational reform, immigration, and global warming become battlegrounds in which correctness and the actual truth fight it out—but with most of the moral leverage seemingly on the side of correctness, which has the power to shame and stigmatize all who oppose it. Correctness constitutes a power in itself, a power substantial enough to prevail easily, much of the time, over the actual truth.

Yet regimes of correctness (even the softer American variety) always stifle the human imagination and lead to cultural stagnation because they are inherently repressive.

They impose an empty and often tyrannical conformity on society. One need only think of communism and socialism in postwar Europe—entire peoples policed into a socialist form of political correctness by autocrats and their henchmen. America, of course, is not Eastern Europe, but many of our institutions are being held in thrall to the idea of moral intimidation as power. Try to get a job today as an unapologetic conservative in the average American university, or in the State Department, or on public radio. The point is that even in "the land of the free," correctness has tentacles of power that reach out and determine the life possibilities of people, opening doors to some and closing them to others. Today our political identities embroil us in a kind of unacknowledged tribalism that transgresses our democratic principles.

In America today our great divide in many ways comes down to a feud between the repressions of correctness, on the one hand, and freedom, on the other. Were correctness to prevail, its know-nothingism and repressiveness would surely lead to cultural decline. Even if freedom offers no guarantee of something better, it is at least freedom, and the possibilities are infinite.

My ambition in this book is not to offer a pat series of solutions that might heal our great divide. We all know, to the point of cliché, what the solutions are: mutual respect, empathy, flexibility, compromise, and so on. I believe that

great democracies—and America can surely count itself a
great democracy—come to divides like this in order to grow
and to reinvent themselves in response to great challenges,
both from their own history and from the contemporary
world they contend with. Because our culture is so habituated to freedom—freedom is our royal endowment—we
don't need revolution. We need the courage to see through
to the bottom of things, to understand, and then to reinvent
ourselves accordingly. Today's great divide comes from a
shallowness of understanding. We don't altogether know
what to do with our history, or how to position ourselves in
the modern world. So everything is a squabble. Our fights
are ferocious both between and within our political parties.
No doubt this culture war will continue until time and
struggle pile up more evidence on one side than the other.
History will finally arbitrate.

The goal of this essay, therefore, is not to find solutions
to the problems as much as to understand them.

2

A Collision

IN EARLY 1965, Daniel Patrick Moynihan, then an assistant secretary of labor, published a landmark study: *The Negro Family: The Case for National Action*. In it he wrote that blacks had come a long way toward winning their civil rights, but that further progress was now likely to be stymied by the dramatic increase in female-headed households among blacks. Moynihan's implication was clear: although plainly this family breakdown had its source in centuries of inhumane treatment, it was nevertheless now essentially a black problem. In other words, there were clear cultural patterns within the black community itself—having nothing to do with racism or discrimination in the 1960s—that would keep blacks from achieving true parity with whites.

Moynihan was immediately called a racist by much of America's intellectual establishment for "blaming the victim," and his report quickly sank into oblivion. Worse, he became an object lesson to all social scientists, so that almost no research implying black responsibility for black problems was done for the next twenty years—this even as the problem of female-headed households proliferated to the point of generating a vast black underclass in America.

Moynihan's mistake was to put literal truth on a collision course with liberalism's poetic truth. His research had been superb, and history has shown that his conclusions were nothing less than prophetic. Since the mid-1960s when he so explicitly identified the problem, family breakdown has blossomed into arguably the single worst problem black America faces. And, just as Moynihan predicted, it spawned countless other problems in black America, including gang violence, drug abuse, low academic achievement, high dropout and unemployment rates, and high crime and incarceration rates. Moynihan's literal truth—that family breakdown would stymie black advancement even as racism and discrimination declined—is simply irrefutable today, nearly fifty years after his report.

But over all these decades, liberalism's prevailing poetic truth has been that blacks are eternal victims: their problems are always the result of some determinism, some unfairness or injustice that impinges on them like an ongoing rain out of permanently hostile skies. And in the white liberal imagination, blacks are *only* victims. Liberalism expresses its inborn racism in the way it overlooks the full human complexity of blacks—the fact that they are more than mere victims—in order to distill and harden the idea of their victimization into a currency of liberal power.

When Moynihan pointed to black family breakdown as a barrier to black progress, he was showing blacks to be more than victims. Here was a grey area, he implied, in which the problem—a rise in female-headed households—was more a legacy of past oppression than the result of ongoing oppression. It was a residue of the past; but, even if all racism and discrimination suddenly disappeared, the problem itself would still exist. And if government programs and public policy incentives were created to encourage family cohesion, it would still fall on blacks to achieve that cohesion. In other words, their victimization—past or present—would never spare them responsibility for the problem.

Moynihan did not say all this directly; his work simply took it for granted as a commonplace in human affairs that victims must live with what has happened to them, so that, despite the cosmic unfairness of it all, responsibility for struggling with weaknesses caused by their victimization ultimately falls on them. This was the realism that caused Moynihan to collide with liberalism's poetic truth.

The new liberalism that emerged in the 1960s actually coveted responsibility for black problems—or at least the illusion of responsibility—because there was so much moral and political power in the idea of delivering blacks from their tragic past. This was the font of power that enabled Lyndon Johnson to launch—in the middle of an economically prosperous decade—his Great Society and War on Poverty initiatives (the word "poverty" standing in here as code for black poverty).

The speech that offered the rationale for these outsized initiatives was delivered in 1965 at Howard University, the nation's premier black university. And this famous speech was infused with allusions to slavery and segregation, as if President Johnson knew that his mandate for a New Deal–like expansion of government would derive from his willingness to own up to these American shames. These shames were his power. "You do not," he said, "take a person who, for years, has been hobbled by chains and liberate him, bring him up to the starting line of a race and then say, 'you are free to compete with all others,' and still justly believe that you have been completely fair."

In the end, Moynihan's unpardonable sin was to threaten liberal power by working from the assumption that blacks could be the agents of their own fates despite all the victimization they had endured. President Johnson's speech (a speech that remains the clearest articulation ever of post-1960s liberalism) positioned the government to be the agent of black uplift. Johnson rationalized his position with the poetic truth that blacks were always and only victims. This reductionism dehumanized blacks, but it served liberal power perfectly. In claiming to uplift blacks—and thus to redeem America's shame—liberalism could claim a moral authority that translated into real political power. And this is how blacks came to be "mined" by liberalism for the power inherent in their legacy of victimization. Moynihan's truth, on the other hand, was too literal and too complex to serve liberal power. Thus his report is now famous, both for its extraordinary prescience and for the speed with which it was dispatched.

IN THE 1960s, a certain cultural unity went out of American life. Moynihan had done his work assuming that it was still in place. He would have assumed, for example, that most people accepted—as a commonplace—that oppression might well cause certain pathologies in its victims. But by 1965 this was no longer a commonplace. Already a new liberalism was beginning to reshape the meaning of things. This liberalism rejected the whole idea that female-headed households *meant* black pathology. Instead it argued that such households only reflected a more matriarchal family system among blacks—an echo of the African past—in which boys found plenty of male role models in their extended families. Moreover, it argued that black difficulties stemmed from oppression in the present, not from pathologies bred by past oppression. Whether such claims were true or not didn't matter so much. This new liberalism was on a kind of tear, and it argued—in area after area of American life—that things did not mean what we had always thought they meant.

Liberalism came on in the 1960s as a revolution in meaning. Old narratives of meaning were being upended everywhere. Picture, for example, a beautifully coifed and white-gloved suburban housewife in the early 1960s standing next to a gleaming new Buick or Oldsmobile in the driveway of her sun-splashed California tract house, three well-scrubbed children at her side. Is this woman the perfect emblem of female fulfillment in America's postwar prosperity, or is she in fact a victim, a soul smothered by an American propriety that systemically subjugates women? Or picture an army general, rolled sleeves and dark glasses, driving through the streets of Saigon in an open jeep. Is he a heroic defender of freedom in a cold war against communist tyranny, or is he an imperialist and white supremacist bent on exploiting a Third World people? Or think of a Black Panther in the late 1960s shooting it out with the "pigs." Is he simply a thug defying legitimate authority, or does legitimacy lie with him as a man bravely confronting his oppressor?

In the 1960s, liberalism began to offer new narratives of meaning so that the members of almost every group came to have a politicized idea of themselves. And all these narratives were conceived in reaction to the great shames of America's past—racism, sexism, territorial conquest (manifest destiny), corporate greed, militarism, and so on. Before the 1960s, if blacks or women were discriminated against, or otherwise made to live as second-class citizens, the implication was that they were somehow inferior. But in the 1960s a new idea blossomed: that despite its greatness, America was guilty of profound injustice. This meant that the "inferiority" of blacks and women was not a natural law but a fabrication, a construct, conceived to justify their victimization. In other words, the meaning of "inferiority" changed from something that was the victim's fault to something that was the oppressor's fault. Inferiority was not inferiority; it was a disparity that was the measure of oppression. So the liberal narratives of the 1960s gave us a new way of comprehending America: this nation that was a beacon of freedom to the world was also a nation that had relentlessly oppressed more than half its citizens.

Through this new lens of meaning, the housewife with the white gloves was a woman made to live within a cage of subtle misogynistic repressions that reduced her to kitsch, a Norman Rockwell image of prosperity and domestic contentment. The army general was surely an unreconstructed imperialist, cruising the streets of Saigon disdainful of the yellow people he was called upon to defend. And the Black Panther shooting it out with the "pigs" was a latter-day Che Guevara, a figure embodying the glamour of revolution as he battles the police in his beret and black leather jacket. In this new and darker conception of America, there is a broad template that stamps out two kinds of people: they are either victims of America's shames or victimizers who perpetrate those shames.

Post-1960s liberalism made this template one of its central poetic truths. It built its credibility on the assumption that America was simply given to victimizing blacks, women, gays, consumers, workers, inner-city school children, the environment, and so on. And surely America was in fact guilty of much victimization. Yet, even after America became aware of many of its habits of victimization and began to evolve away from them, this liberalism insisted that the impulse to victimize was still an essential feature of the American character.

Insistence on poetic truth is the methodology—if not the essence—of post-1960s liberalism. This liberalism is an ideology and a politics of ugly givens (America is racist; America is militaristic; America is sexist), and it seeks power in the name of overcoming these givens with little regard for whether they are actually true. Its fundamental corruption is that it demands power commensurate with the hyperbole of its poetic truths. And today—after fifty years of real moral evolution in America—these poetic truths are indeed hyperbolic.

Liberalism in the twenty-first century is, for the most part, a moral manipulation that exaggerates inequity and unfairness in American life in order to justify overreaching public policies and programs. This liberalism is, for example, not much interested in addressing discrimination case by case; rather, it assumes that all minorities and women are systemically discriminated against so that only government-enforced preferential policies for these groups—across the entire society—can bring us close to equity. In health care, for example, the poetic truth of systemic inequality means that government-mandated health care is the only way to fairness. The point is that the exaggerations of poetic truth—here the claim of a deep and permanent American inclination to inequality—redefine social equality away from equal opportunity and toward an idealism in which equality can only be engineered by the government.

This liberalism is invested in an overstatement of America's present sinfulness based on the nation's past sins. It conflates the past into the present so that the present is indistinguishable from the ugly past. And so modern liberalism is grounded in a paradox: it tries to be "progressive" and forward looking by fixing its gaze backward. It insists that America's shameful past is the best explanation of its current social problems. It looks at the present, but it sees only the past.

THE ADVENT OF THIS political and cultural liberalism in the 1960s plunged America into what has been called a "culture war." But it would probably be more accurate to call it a cold war. "Culture war" implies a struggle between two factions within a common culture—a struggle to reform or redefine a broad cultural commonality. But this is a "war" between two foes—today's political Right and Left—that are almost as fundamentally antithetical and irreconcilable as the Soviet Union and the United States once were. Both sides feel existentially threatened by the other, which means that their war is not about the negotiation of a new commonality encompassing elements of both sides; rather, each side seeks total victory over the other—the ideological annihilation of the other.

In this environment, real moderation is all but impossible because, for both sides, moderation feels like ideological suicide. And in fact there is no clear middle ground between today's Right and Left. People on both sides exclaim moderation as a high virtue, but today they whistle in the dark. Where is the middle road between Maynard Keynes and Milton Friedman? What would moderation between such polar opposites look like? How would the principle of government spending to stimulate the economy moderate with the principle of less government spending to stimulate the economy? When one side is traveling east and the other west, how do you trade a little east for a little west?

The young man in Aspen and I were headed in opposite directions. We were forty years removed from the 1960s—that decade in which America began to seriously move away from so many of its past sins—and there was simply no middle ground between us. What we had in common—our broad agreement that racism, sexism, military adventurism, and other forms of injustice were wrong—did nothing to assuage the absoluteness of our ideological differences.

3

Hypocrisy

I T BEGAN IN HYPOCRISY.

My sport as a kid was swimming. I loved the very medium of water the first time I waded neck deep into a creek at summer camp. Instinctively I knew how to breathe in it and move through it. I started competitive swimming at age eight, and was first-string varsity in breaststroke and individual medley as a freshman in high school.

But in my junior year I came to a little crisis of faith with swimming. It is a grueling sport. Practice every day was to find one's pain threshold and push through it. I envied my friends on the basketball team who actually played a *game*. In swimming you mortified yourself. My attention began to drift to other things, and at season's end, I did not even qualify for the state meet.

Still, I was elected team captain for the upcoming year, and I was thought to be the team's best hope for a medal at the next year's state meet. So at the sad end of my junior year, I determined—in a kind of covenant with myself—that I would get refocused over the summer, and come back in the fall ready to give 110 percent.

But on the first day of the fall semester—my senior year—I ran into a teammate in the registration line. We had swum together since we'd been eight years old. I thought there would be no more than a casual hello, since we would see each other soon enough at preseason swim practice. But he was so anxious to tell me about his fabulous summer that he begged the girl behind me to cut in line. And I will never forget the innocent exhilaration with which he told me a story that I took in like a fist in the gut. He and the entire varsity team—except for me, the team's captain, best swimmer, and only black—had spent three weeks at our coach's family summerhouse on Lake Michigan. They'd had a ball, swimming all day in the lake as well as in the coach's pool, fishing, barbequing, and practical joking after dark. And then there were the girls from surrounding summerhouses. The team, he said, had bonded like never before, and everyone was coming back to school fired up and ready to give everything for our greatest season ever. It was just too bad that I'd had to work and couldn't be there.

Of course I had never been invited to the coach's summerhouse on the lake. I knew nothing about what had to have been an elaborately coordinated team excursion. Moreover, not a single teammate—many of whom I had swum with for almost a decade by then—had even hinted to me all summer long that such a holiday was in the offing. I had worked in the Chicago stockyards that summer, so while I was rolling two-hundred-pound barrels of beef kidneys—swimming in cow piss and destined for the kidney pies of England—up to the packing line, they and their families (whom I also knew) were arranging this happy summer interlude on the lake without me.

All these white people—the coach, my teammates, and their families—would have comprised a little community of coconspirators that, all together, invented the rationalizations necessary to exclude the only black swimmer on the team. White lies, as it were, would have been told all around. When my teammate approached me in the registration line so anxious to tell me about his summer, I could see—even as a teenager—that his very exuberance was the repression of some inner doubt or guilt. It was one of those self-serving circumlocutions that racism thrives on. Because he believed himself to be innocent of racism, he (and the other coconspirators) reasoned that he could never have had so much fun if he had known himself to be complicit with racism. Therefore, if he had great fun, it was proof that he had not conspired to exclude his black teammate. He wanted me to witness his excitement as proof of his innocence.

But I would have happily abandoned the stockyards and the beef kidneys marinating in cow piss for a few weeks on the beaches of Lake Michigan in the summertime. My parents—also known by all these white people—would not have begrudged me this fun. But no invitation had been forthcoming. So there I stood in the registration line, expected to share in my friend's happiness over a great good time that he had colluded in excluding me from—and for no other reason than my race.

Yet I had made a covenant with myself to make this a great year. And there was the possibility of a swimming scholarship to a Big Ten university. (I had already visited one such campus.) I had something to gain by casting off this racial snub—a commonplace, after all, in the still segregated America of the early 1960s.

A month later, on the first day of practice for the new season, I dove into the water determined to go forward with my covenant to swim harder and with more focus than ever before. In that first dive my body aligned perfectly to slit the water for the shallowest possible entry, and I was happy to see that my old form was still there. Even in this first warm-up lap I was going for speed, and almost immediately I was at the other end. But instead of flipping the turn and pushing off for the next lap, I stopped abruptly and stood up, planting my feet squarely on the tiled bottom of the pool.

A powerful clarity had suddenly come over me, and I was stilled by it. Clearly it had been building inside me for some time and had simply found this moment—this very first lap of the thousands of laps to come in the new season—to break into my consciousness. And it gave me peace. I stood there for a long time, waist deep in the shallow end of my high-school swimming pool, perfectly calm yet stunned to realize that I would never swim competitively again.

And I knew this definitively. I was done with this sport that had given me so much—self-esteem, a work ethic, and—the current racial snub notwithstanding—a chance to see a little of the world beyond my segregated black neighborhood. But, standing there in the water, I knew that the covenant with myself to swim harder had only been prelude to letting go. What stopped me in the water that day was the realization that I had already quit the sport of swimming, that I had been quitting without admitting it to myself for over a year by then. I had become interested in other things. I couldn't have articulated it then, but quitting swimming felt like an act of loyalty to a new idea of possibility—so much so that to continue swimming would have felt cowardly.

But I knew my coach wouldn't see it that way. I knew he would think I was quitting because of the way he and the team had snubbed me over the past summer. And I also knew that he would fly into a rage. And that is exactly what he did.

He said that I was running away from my responsibilities as team captain. I was a fool to let a little thing like the team's summer interlude put me off swimming. Yes, his mother, who owned the summerhouse on the lake, was surely a bigot. But so what? He wasn't; nor were my teammates. Why did I want to embarrass them? Hadn't he personally driven me to visit the swimming program at a Big Ten university? Hadn't he made it clear that this was to be "our year"—since a swimming scholarship would help him as well as me? Why let his "old-fashioned" mother come between me and swimming?

But, of course, for me, his mother had nothing to do with it. I would never have quit swimming because of her snub. I quit, with nothing but gratitude toward the sport, simply because I had come to the end of my passion for it. I actually liked the coach, and I think he liked me. We had had adventures together. On the way home from our Big Ten visit, his car had broken down, forcing us to hitchhike the last hundred miles—me especially grateful because, as a young white man, he could easily catch a ride and make the necessary excuses for his black companion.

But in his office on that afternoon when our relationship ended, there was only a great gulf between us. He ranted and I angerlessly defended myself. I was amazed to see that I had lost all fear of him.

———————

ONE GREAT DIFFERENCE between evil and hypocrisy is that people can live rather easily with the former but not with the latter. Evil—and complicity with evil—is usually done under the cover of numerous rationalizations that declare the evil to be everything but what it is. But hypocrisy is *established* when evil is clearly visible through the fog of rationalization—when rationalization is seen for what it is. So hypocrisy is not an act of evil; it is the pretense of innocence even as one is clearly in league with evil, and with all the duplicities and deceptions that serve evil.

Evil, in fact, is often rewarded (Hitler almost succeeded, slave owners thrived for centuries); but hypocrisy, once it is established as fact for all to see, always punishes rather than rewards. The exposed hypocrite is shrouded in an aura of ignominy and disrepute. His moral authority and power start to crumble. He is now known to have somehow trafficked in the convenience of evil, and all his self-justifications come to seem outrageous affronts to reason.

———————

THIS WAS THE AURA OF HYPOCRISY that began to settle over my coach on that afternoon when I walked away from swimming. He was not bothered much by his complicity with his mother's evil—the fact that he had orchestrated a little racial conspiracy among my teammates and their families in order to abide by her evil. There were rationalizations aplenty to cover that. He could likely have gone for the rest of his life untroubled by what he had done. But as I sat there in his office, still wet from the pool, I was—whether I intended to be or not—the worst sort of threat to him: as the "victim" of his evil, I had the power to refute all his rationalizations, and thus to establish him as a hypocrite for all to see. I had the power to diminish him in the eyes of the world as well as in his own eyes.

So he tried to turn the tables. He implied that I was the one who was "hung up" on race. With a raised eyebrow he wondered if I wasn't becoming a "black militant" (a new and terrifying term to whites in the 1960s). Were my parents—well known locally for their civil rights activities—encouraging me in this? And by then he had an audience. Half the team had left the pool to listen outside the door that he had left fully open.

I had only wanted to go home and rejoin life without swimming. I had no memory of life without the burden of competitive swimming, and I was ecstatic at the prospect of laying that burden down. But it was now clear that I would have to fight the race issue to get out of that office. So, speaking loudly enough for my eavesdropping teammates to hear, I said, "Well coach, the truth is that you did go along with your racist mother, didn't you? She said no blacks, and you made sure there were no blacks. You organized the whole team and their families to exclude me simply because I'm black. And you knew me . . . personally. We spent time together. I babysat your son. And you did it anyway." Then I said it quietly, almost respectfully, "You and everybody on this team are racists."

This did it. His eyes widened in shock. A lifetime of rationalizations had sheltered him from the idea of himself as a racist, and now he was astonished to hear himself bluntly described as one. It was a term that linked him to the lowest rung of white society—the Klan, white ethnics in northern cities, George Wallace standing in the schoolhouse door, white mobs screaming and spitting at black children on their way to school. His family was well to do. He would never have imagined himself in such company.

In the early 1960s, white America had not yet fully absorbed the idea that complicity with segregation was what made segregation possible, so that mere compliance carried the same moral culpability as advocating for segregation. My coach, like so many white Americans in that era, was blindsided by this raising of the moral bar. In complying with his mother's racist edict, he no doubt thought he was simply observing propriety—following an age-old "good manners" of race relations in which his exclusion of me had nothing to do with racial malice but rather with a "civilized" desire to spare everyone embarrassment. When I called him a racist, I shocked him with what was then still a novel idea in race relations: that racism thrived by passing itself off as a kind of decency, a noblesse oblige.

I will never forget the "movie" of emotions that played across his face—the way his smirking suspicion of me as a "black militant" collapsed, was followed by a moment of stupefaction, and then a longer moment that I would like to describe as self-recognition but that was more likely simply the realization that he had no rationalizations left. He'd come to the end of self-justification, and to the end of his entitlement as a white—an entitlement that had once allowed any dumb rationalization for white supremacy to fly as truth. He had come to a place where it was no longer possible for him to be two people—the guy who was my coach, mentor, and friend; and the guy who orchestrated a racist conspiracy against me.

I had established his hypocrisy as a fact in the world. I had shown a light on his little evil through the fog of his rationalizations.

When I stood up to leave, I felt a flicker of my old affection for him. He was saving face by looking hurt and betrayed—as if I was the one who had wronged him. In the coming months he would give me this hurt look whenever we passed in the hallways. But it never affected me. I could see that he was afraid. Perhaps he was worried that I would get him in trouble with his higher-ups. In any case, after I left his office that day, we never spoke again.

And on the way out I ran squarely into the cluster of teammates crowded around the door. Like the coach, each of them wanted to explain themselves. Several began to yammer at the same time, offering up little scenarios of self-justification—they'd been on a family vacation and knew nothing about the plot to exclude me; they all believed that I would never like the northern woods anyway; they'd been told that I'd had to work all summer because my family couldn't afford to send me with them. All obvious falsehoods that none of them had ever bothered to check out with me.

It is often the victim's fate to be victimized a second time by the moral neediness of his former victimizer. One can chalk up many of black America's problems since the 1960s precisely to this phenomenon. The larger society around us—having acknowledged its abuse of us—wants to take charge of our fate in order to redeem itself, thus smothering us in social programs and policies that rob us of full autonomy all over again. Once my coach's and my teammates' hypocrisy was clear even to themselves, they all of a sudden needed me vastly more than I needed them. All moral authority had shifted to me, so that I—unexpectedly—had the power to pronounce on their fundamental human decency. Having colluded in the evil of excluding me (a small betrayal as it related to me, but a profound betrayal as it related to the American creed of fairness, honor, and equality), they had inadvertently bestowed on me the priestly power of dispensation.

All of a sudden my old teammates were my petitioners and I was their moral magistrate. They formed into a chattering chorus that followed me from the coach's office, through the shower, and into the locker room, where they yammered at me even as I dressed. In the weeks and months to come, many of them would come alongside me and press the case for their innocence all over again. Others followed the coach's lead: I had betrayed the team and undermined their season. I was to be shunned. I didn't like either of these roles any more than they liked being reduced to racists. We had grown up together, traveled together, and yet here we were.

After that afternoon, every one of those people was lost to me—and vice versa. I remember finally breaking free of them outside the locker room and walking home alone. And once alone, I had no energy for judging them. I remember that sudden and sweet solitude. Alone—and free of the harangue of white moral neediness—I could look up and think for a moment. Such a heavy and wearying moral arithmetic sits upon race relations in America.

It was an unseasonably cold evening, well below freezing, when I finally bolted from my petitioners and walked home. But I never noticed the cold until I got home and stepped through the back door into my mother's warm kitchen. She looked at me and laughed, then she reached out and touched my head. "Your hair is frozen solid, hard as a rock. You're supposed to dry off after you leave the pool."

4

The Moral Asymmetry of Hypocrisy

I TELL THE ABOVE STORY TO ILLUSTRATE A POINT: that in the 1960s, the moral authority of the United States—the world's greatest and most powerful postwar nation—was suddenly diminished in the eyes of many Americans, just as the moral authority of my swimming coach was diminished in my eyes on that long-ago afternoon. In the 1960s, America underwent what can only be described as an archetypal "fall"—a descent from "innocence" into an excruciating and inescapable self-knowledge.

This innocence had always been a delusion. It was far more a cultivated ignorance of America's sins than innocence of them, and this ignorance was helped along by a culturally embedded pattern of rationalizations, bigotries, stereotypes, and lies. But all this came under profound challenge in the 1960s as one form of American hypocrisy after another—everything from racism and the second-class treatment of women to Vietnam and our neglect of the environment—came to light and further cracked the veneer of American innocence.

These hypocrisies had been a part of American life forever, and the justifications that covered them up had hardened over time into a conventional wisdom. In the 1950s, many whites said, as if uttering a sad but immutable truth, "Segregation is nature's way; people will always stick with their own kind," or "We don't hate blacks; we just want them to go slow." (The great southern novelist William Faulkner, who had written some of the most finely drawn black characters in all of American literature, became a famous exponent of the "go slow" argument.) Well into the 1960s, this conventional wisdom had it that women should not be admitted to graduate or professional schools because they would only take seats away from deserving males, then marry, get pregnant, and abandon the profession altogether. In the "gray flannel suit" world of postwar corporate America, there was outward conformity to traditional sexual mores, even as the first stirrings of the sexual revolution were everywhere apparent.

The civil rights movement established racism as the premier American hypocrisy—our oldest and most unabidable disgrace. But after racism, it was the Vietnam War (full-fledged feminism came soon after) that began to entrench the idea of American hypocrisy. Here was America's first truly ambiguous war—a war that confused, divided, and wearied the American people from its beginning to its end. Here was the greatest power on earth fighting a full-tilt war against a tiny Third World nation 5,000 miles off its shore—and supporting this undertaking with a universal draft, billions of dollars, and ultimately more than 50,000 American casualties.

Whatever one may think of the Vietnam War today, it startled an entire generation of young Americans in the 1960s with the idea that cynicism and hypocrisy were the central characteristics of America's "military-industrial complex." It was the grandfatherly President Dwight D. Eisenhower— a Republican with legendary military credentials—who warned us of this danger. Yet here we were in Vietnam claiming to be fighting in defense of freedom, while behind the scenes we were trying to puppeteer the South Vietnamese government—even to the point of clandestinely arranging for the assassination of the country's uncooperative leader (General Ngo Dinh Diem). And if freedom defined our mission 5,000 miles away in Vietnam, why was freedom for blacks at home so difficult to achieve? So, as the war dramatically escalated, it also escalated the legend of American hypocrisy—or what Senator J. William Fulbright (D-AR) called America's "arrogance of power."

There was simply no credible way for the American government to frame the Vietnam War as a noble or necessary application of American power. There was no inspiring idealism at stake in this war for Americans beyond a vague anticommunism. And certainly Americans did not feel that either victory or defeat in this remote war would much affect their way of life. It was at best a tactical war, a chess move within the larger Cold War against the Soviet Union and China. It was driven by geopolitical calculation rather than passion or idealism or necessity. Thus it failed to inspire Americans.

Still, it demanded a sacrifice of blood and treasure commensurate with great transformative wars; it asked Americans to fight in Vietnam as if our nation's fate hung in the balance, when in fact it did not. And this goes to the core of the Vietnam War's hypocrisy: the government tried to pass off a tactical war hardly worth fighting as if it were a transformative war of national survival. This put the government in the position of relentlessly "spinning" the American people.

And it was this constant spinning of the war—the rosy scenarios of progress on the ground; the inflated enemy casualty numbers; the Orwellian doublespeak; Secretary of Defense Melvin Laird referring to a new bomb as a "protective reaction missile"; or officials saying we were fire-bombing villages in the name of "pacification"—that began to expand the legend of American hypocrisy exponentially. Underlying all this government hyping of a dubious war was the universal draft, which effectively forced all Americans into a serious consideration of the war. All American males at the age of eighteen had to avail themselves to the prosecution of war. This gave their mothers, fathers, relations, friends, and communities an immediate stake in the meaning of the war. If the war itself plunged America into self-examination, the universal draft added a life-and-death dimension to this inward look.

So here was a divisive, unpopular, and, in many ways, hypocritical war that the government ordered America's young men to fight. Possibly this war would have resonated differently in America had it not come so closely on the heels of the 1960s civil rights movement. The Korean War—another remote and draining war that came before the civil rights revolution—was not divisive in the same way that the Vietnam War was. But by the 1960s the civil rights movement had established the idea of American hypocrisy across the entire world. Images of water hoses and police dogs attacking middle-aged black women who were marching peacefully for the most basic of civil and human rights were broadcast around the globe. Certainly the world had long known of this feature of American life, but in the age of film, television, and photographic journalism, the world was made to witness it. The civil rights movement was an international story precisely because it revealed stunning hypocrisy at the heart of the world's oldest and greatest democracy. It put the lie to the American experiment in freedom.

The Vietnam War quickly came to seem of a fabric with America's hypocritical nature. It revealed a headstrong government pushing ahead with a war that no one wanted—a government straining to codify its empty rationalizations for war ("containment," "the domino theory," "fighting for freedom") as conventional wisdom so that people would reflexively go along with the war. The Vietnam War showed us a coercive American government. This was not the America of World War II, in which citizens were called to arms against a profound enemy; this was an America in which citizens were coerced into arms against a negligible enemy.

It was this coercion that began to radicalize mainstream white America far more than the civil rights movement ever had. After all, segregation disaffected blacks and minorities, but not necessarily whites. And while it is true that there was an emerging white disaffection in the 1950s—the beatniks, the highbrow socialist intellectuals, the remnants of a communist underground from the 1930s, and the whites who simply identified with the civil rights movement—it was the Vietnam War that first gave the sons and daughters of the great American middle class the feeling that their government was dealing with them in bad faith.

––––––––––

So THE VIETNAM WAR—on the heels of the civil rights movement—did something profound: it introduced anti-Americanism as a new and *legitimate* source of moral authority within society. It bifurcated American authority. There was the traditional "mainstream" authority, in which America, even if racist, was always right in the wars it fought. Here unconditional love of country was always the test of one's Americaness. Yes, we were a democracy and therefore free to live as individuals, but in matters of war we pulled together—even across racial lines—with something close to absolutism.

With the Vietnam War, the government was clearly exploiting the reflexive loyalty of the American people by demanding the heroic sacrifices of true patriotism in a cause that was spurious, at best. And without a clear equivalency between the importance of "the cause" and the sacrifices required to defend it—an equivalency that had been so obvious in World War II—the government could only cajole and muscle its own people. It could only manufacture an importance commensurate with the sacrifices it was demanding. In other words, it could only lie.

It was the *pretended* importance of the Vietnam War that quickly turned it into a glaring instance of American hypocrisy.

And this helped to spawn a brand new "countercultural" idea of moral authority. "Authenticity" became an emblematic word in the 1960s, a word cast in opposition to America's hypocrisy and inauthenticity. The Vietnam War was inauthentic; resistance to the war was the very essence of a new countercultural authenticity.

———

AND THEN THERE WAS FEMINISM. No movement that came to the fore in the 1960s was more culturally transformative than the women's movement for equality. Like the antiwar movement, the women's movement took the idea of American hypocrisy to the masses, to white women as well as to women of every color and socioeconomic background. America had relegated women to second-class status throughout its history, not even granting them the right to vote (the Nineteenth Amendment) until 1920, almost 150 years after the nation's founding as the world's first democracy. So in the 1960s, this old and patronizing American hypocrisy came starkly and irrepressibly to light. And, accordingly, the word "sexism" took its place alongside "racism" as an old and infamous American scourge that would no longer be tolerated.

So now women, along with minorities, were effectively in the same position that I was in on that long-ago afternoon when I sat across the desk from my high-school swimming coach—they too had lost their fear. There is a compelling dialectic at work when hypocrisies become established and can no longer be denied: they elicit fearlessness in the people who have been victimized by them. Women had protested their second-class status in one form or another since before the American Revolution. (Abigail Adams had admonished her husband, John Adams, on his way to the Constitutional Convention, to make sure he secured the vote for women in the new constitution, but of course he did not.)

But by the late 1960s, women simply would no longer be denied. Like blacks, they forced America into a reckoning—a complete renegotiation of their position and role in every aspect of American life, from the protocols of business and politics to family life. They insisted on parity with men in the workplace as well as in the family. They would work outside the home if they chose to do so, and they would expect men to take up new responsibilities within the home—greater participation in everything from childrearing to cooking and cleaning. They transformed the institution of marriage, moving the norm away from gender-designated responsibilities and toward shared responsibilities. And they made the larger point that gender must never again be an occasion for hierarchy.

As if to echo the women's revolution, the sexual revolution followed close on its heels—one more "liberation" movement seeking to free Americans from the tyranny of small-mindedness, in this case the hypocrisy of an antiquated sexual propriety. With both "the pill" and abortion readily available (even before *Roe v. Wade*), the angst, repression, and duplicity surrounding sex came to seem a little preposterous. The liberationist spirit of the times—combined with the legalization of abortion and birth control's promise to spare women unwanted pregnancies—seemed to overcome what many had casually accepted for women as a biological mandate to second-class citizenship.

Conventional wisdom always had it that sexual liberation would only make women more vulnerable. But as the 1960s progressed, sexual freedom amounted to a grant of equality to women. To be against the sexual revolution was, in effect, to be against full equality. And the prudish sexual mores of the past that claimed to "protect" women came to be seen as a double standard that actually subjugated women in a "patriarchal" society. These mores were seen as hypocrisies that left women "barefoot and pregnant" while men roamed free in the world. So the sexual revolution shared a first principle with the women's movement: that women themselves—rather than some patriarchal social or moral order—must always be "in charge of their own bodies." This is how the decriminalization of abortion became the first brick in the foundation of female equality.

To be "pro-choice" was to be for the complete equality of women, because it surrendered to women complete sovereignty over their lives. To be against abortion was to diminish that sovereignty, and thus, to slide back into the hypocrisy of sexism.

———————

THEN, ALSO IN THE 1960S, came the beginnings of the environmental movement. Rachel Carson's *Silent Spring*, first published in 1962, revealed that even America's splendid environment could be "victimized" in ways not unlike the victimization of blacks and women. All over America the chemical detritus of the industrial age was allowed to seep into the earth and to pollute the rivers and streams. "The chemical war is never won," Carson said. "All life is caught in its violent crossfire."

Carson wrote *Silent Spring* while fighting breast cancer, a condition she suspected had been brought on by exposure to chemical and radiation waste. Her own circumstance echoed her larger point: that environmental indifference ultimately victimized human beings. This melded her work into the 1960s template of protest writing in which a callous, white "patriarchy" exploited innocents for profit.

So the issue of the environment entered the American consciousness as yet another great American hypocrisy. America's natural beauty and vast natural resources had always been a source of national pride ("America the Beautiful"). Yet, just as we celebrated our love of equality even as we betrayed it, we celebrated our natural bounty even as we despoiled it. *Silent Spring* was a transformative book in the 1960s, like *Uncle Tom's Cabin* had been in the nineteenth century, because it exposed a flagrant American hypocrisy. It showed America, once again, to be cloaking itself in innocence (as it had done around slavery, segregation, women's rights, and its recent wars) to conceal an underlying evil—in this case, a disregard of the environment out of a lust for gain at any cost.

All these 1960s movements sought to move America beyond its habit of hypocrisy and self-congratulation. I don't believe these movements wanted to undermine America so much as to bring America to account for its hubris, its "arrogance of power"—a temptation that comes with great power wherever it emerges. They didn't want a revolution as much as they wanted America, in all its self-evident greatness, to find the humility and discipline to live within the principles of its own Constitution. They wanted a humbling.

Ultimately, these movements came to have their own excesses, their own "arrogance of power." They all went too far. Knowing that they spoke out of a genuine historical grievance, they all too often lapsed into hollow sanctimony. (Think of Al Sharpton or Jesse Jackson or any number of shrill feminists or zealous environmentalists.) Still, it was these movements that did in fact humble and transform America. And that older *pre*-1960s liberalism, grounded in individual freedom, can be proud of this fact. It made the point that America could not go back to hypocrisy as a way of life.

5

The Compounding of Hypocrisy

T HE DECADE OF THE 1960s was arguably the most fundamentally transformative decade in American history. It was a period in which virtually all of the country's great hypocrisies (and the movements that gave them visibility) were finally established beyond any doubt. What does it mean to be "established"? It means that the hypocrisy one is protesting against becomes openly acknowledged as a *fact* of life in America. No one seriously disputes its existence anymore. So all the great movements of the 1960s—the women's movement, the civil rights movement, the antiwar movement, and so on—were actually quests for legitimacy.

They wanted the American people as well as the government to say, yes, your grievance against America is legitimate and it deserves redress. Only this hard-won legitimacy opened the way to redress.

The civil rights movement was the first movement in the 1960s to win legitimacy because its charges against America were so blatantly true. All arguments to the contrary came to look strikingly illegitimate. Then the women's movement, the antiwar movement, and even the sexual revolution won broad legitimacy for their assertions of American hypocrisy. Soon a very specific progression emerged that I now see gave form to that last meeting with my swimming coach, just as it gave form to broader America's encounter with its hypocrisies. In the man there was the outline of the country.

———————

WHEN MY COACH WAS CAUGHT OUT IN HIS HYPOCRISY, he suffered a defeat. He was literally stilled by defeat. All he could do was sit there and stare blankly downward at his little desk, which suddenly seemed very little indeed. The American hypocrisy of which he had partaken had been a resource for him, a cultural prerogative that was his special provenance as a white man. But now, even if this prerogative wasn't entirely extinguished, there was no way he could rely on it again in innocence. Worse, if he tried to—if he colluded again with racism simply to ease his way in the world (to stay in the good graces of his mother)—then he would put himself at risk. The world had changed, and his use of racism as a convenience had come to be understood as illegitimate and impermissible. I could have gotten him in trouble even back then, in the early 1960s. He was defeated because the legitimacy of racism had been defeated in the broader culture, even if much actual racism still persisted.

And the legitimacy that racism had lost transferred over to the black grievance against America as a racist society. Suddenly black protest was perfectly legitimate, understandable in every way. So there he was, shrunken by defeat, just as I was swelled up a little by a new and unexpected legitimacy, quietly confident in the knowledge that simple decency in America now required that black protest be recognized as valid. This kind of legitimacy bestows fearlessness. And this is why our encounter so exemplified the larger social forces and tensions at work in the 1960s. Our respective races had lined us up with these forces—even assigned us discrete roles to play—so that we were virtually acting out a script given to us by history.

And in this script, the fearlessness that my civil rights parents had modeled for me was something the entire society was beginning to admire. Conversely, my coach's collusion with racism was more and more visible as the hypocrisy it actually was. My parents had paid a price for their fearlessness. So there was a tinge of guilt when I faced my coach on that afternoon. The fearlessness my parents had been punished for came to me easily, almost glibly, as a gift from history.

As a social force, fearlessness is infectious. The era of the 1960s was triggered by a handful of fearless blacks in the 1950s, who, led by the Reverend Martin Luther King Jr., boycotted the segregated buses of Montgomery, Alabama. Black maids, chauffeurs, and janitors abandoned the buses and walked miles to and from work in protest of the city's "back of the bus" policy for blacks. And when they succeeded in their protest, their fearlessness became exemplary, something even the usually coy black middle class had to respect and emulate. Soon, fearlessness in the fight against racial segregation became an established marker of character. White college students from the North began flooding into the South eager for the chance to show themselves fearless in the face of this oldest of American evils.

There is a kind of circular synergy at work in all this: as the legitimacy of one's cause grows, fearlessness increases exponentially, which, in turn, wins more legitimacy. Blacks could see that their cause was gaining legitimacy because it began to be celebrated around the world. Martin Luther King received the Nobel Peace Prize in 1963. And the movement's adherence to the Gandhian philosophy of non-violent passive resistance added greatly to this legitimacy. By

forsaking violence, protest marches became occasions of un-
bowed moral witness that stood in sharp contrast to the ugly
hatred and violence on display from the white defenders
of Jim Crow. Nonviolence gave black protest a Christ-like
resonance. The images on the evening news of fifty-year-old
black women—dressed as if for church—mowed down by
water cannons and assaulted by police dogs showed black
Americans to be collectively "nailed to the cross," as it were.
Photographed in his Birmingham jail cell—a man jailed
simply for wanting to be free—Martin Luther King became
a modern Christ, a man of unassailable stoicism put upon
by those who know not what they do.

The American civil rights movement—evolving carefully
and inexorably through the 1940s, 1950s, and 1960s—
generated nothing less than a new model of social transformation. The first feature of this model is always a display
of fearlessness—usually more quiet and profound than
spectacular—that suggests an oppressed group has come
to the end of its fear. (In 1955, Rosa Parks, an unassum-
ing black seamstress, refused to relinquish her seat on a
Montgomery bus to a white man because she was just too
tired "to give in"—her exhaustion after a long day's work
thereby lifting her to a kind of valor.) And in this model,
fearlessness is always asserted nonviolently, so that it has
the arresting power of moral witness. This is social transformation that works by the "perpetual motion" interplay

between moral bravery, on the one hand, and the achievement of legitimacy, on the other.

By the mid-1960s this model of social change was a new American archetype. Women, seeing what blacks had done, began to march and even burn their bras in public displays of fearlessness. Migrant farm laborers in California and across the Southwest marched, conducted strikes and boycotts despite their precarious status in America, and in the process they canonized Cesar Chavez, leader of the National Farm Workers Association, as the Hispanic equivalent of Martin Luther King, another charismatic and transformative leader of an aggrieved people. Then there was the antiwar movement, in which the youth of white middle-class America found their "protest" voice. In bold displays of fearlessness (the 1967 march on the Pentagon and the Kent State massacre in 1970), they spawned an era of almost relentless demonstrations, consequently winning more and more legitimacy for the antiwar cause.

A famous and controversial phrase toward the end of the 1960s was: "Woman as nigger." Most blacks hated this phrase because it used "nigger" as the gold standard of human denigration against which all other persecuted groups calibrated their victimization. Here were white feminists—many born to privilege, many more raised in families in which racism flourished around the dinner table—attaching themselves to the moral authority and hard-earned legitimacy of the black struggle. It wasn't that feminists were against the black struggle; it was that they wanted to steal a bit of its thunder, to claim that they were treated like "niggers," too, as a way of establishing the legitimacy of their own cause.

Certainly none of these groups—antiwar activists, women, hippies, other minorities, even the disaffected white middle class—actually wanted to be "niggers"; they only wanted to *qualify* as "niggers." They wanted access to the same model of social transformation—the "perpetual motion" interplay between fearless protest and legitimacy—that had succeeded in bringing even "niggers" into an almost ascendant legitimacy.

———

THESE GROUPS WANTED to be in the position that I had been in so long ago with my swimming coach. That encounter had been banal on the surface—a high-school kid quitting the team; a swimming coach caught out in an embarrassment. And yet history had given that moment a much broader significance. In betraying me that previous summer—setting up a swim vacation only for my white teammates—he had acted out of an idea of decency that had once enjoyed considerable moral authority in American life. After all, he was white. And being white had always required a certain ingenuity: for the sake of graciousness, if nothing else, one was expected to find ways around any awkward mingling of the races to save everyone embarrassment. But on the afternoon of our encounter, this ingenuity damned him, aligned him with the hypocrisy of "good manners" as the helpmate of evil.

The defeat so visible on the coach's face that afternoon was also America's defeat in the 1960s. What was this defeat? It was an abrupt loss of moral and cultural authority that had to feel—for America as for my coach—like a great vacuum had suddenly opened up in the world. An authority that one had taken for granted, and built a moral identity around, was simply no longer there. White America was like a man who had been leaning rakishly on a fireplace mantle, chatting amicably with friends, when suddenly the mantle had simply collapsed, and he found himself flailing in midair against gravity itself. There was clearly no longer much legitimate support in the culture for the act of excluding a kid from a summer vacation simply because he was black, and then rationalizing it as the only decent thing to do.

For America in the 1960s, there was no longer any legitimate support for that dark streak of hypocrisy that had allowed for racial oppression, sexism, and sometimes an arrogance of power abroad (Vietnam). To the contrary, there was only an abrupt experience of shame and delegitimization.

In that era, a remarkable convergence occurred: So many hypocrisies were established as *legitimate* complaints against America that the nation fell into arguably the worst crisis of moral and cultural authority in its history. How could a society that literally used bigotry as a mechanism of social organization—while claiming to be a democracy devoted to the freedom of every individual—have the moral authority to enforce even the rule of law? Wasn't the rule of law itself so stained with hypocrisy that there was more honor in resisting it than in submitting to it? And didn't this suddenly broken authority have much to do with the epidemic of race riots in the 1960s—riots that left inner cities from Los Angeles to Detroit to Newark smoldering in warlike devastation? Didn't it explain the swift escalation of the antiwar movement into more and more confrontation and violence, so that by the late 1960s a small cadre of middle- and upper-middle-class white youths had become out and out terrorists and revolutionaries? The American Civil War had been a war against secession and slavery—two unambiguous threats to American democracy. But the 1960s launched a war against a quality of the American character: hypocrisy—a universal human weakness, surely, but one made more conspicuous in America precisely because of the self-congratulation with which Americans embraced their creed of freedom and equality.

It is almost impossible to overstate the importance of this collapse of authority. I remember that as the 1960s advanced, there began to be a consciousness, especially among young people, that almost no traditional authority was entirely legitimate (all people "over thirty" were suspect). By 1968 you could question virtually anything. You could question your religion; the "relevance" of a college education; the value of monogamy in marriage; the draconian laws against drug use; a college curriculum grounded solely in Western civilization; the military draft; capitalism itself; the taboos against interracial marriage and homosexuality; the view of pregnancy as an absolute commandment to give birth; the presumed happiness to be found in pleasant suburbs with good schools and lush shade trees weeping into the streets; the faith that industrialization and technological advancements always make for a better life; and so on.

After all, if the 1960s made one overriding point, it was that our great principles and traditions had not saved us from our hypocrisies. If our Declaration of Independence and our Constitution, with all its brilliant amendments spelling out a precise discipline of freedom, were the greatest articulations of democratic principles ever written, they had in fact given us only a stunted democracy in which millions languished outside the circle of full freedom. Here again, my swimming coach—sitting there feeling a vacuum where he had just felt such a confident authority—was emblematic of America. Nature abhors a vacuum, and it was the abrupt and radical decline of America's moral authority in the 1960s that literally called so many long-repressed segments of society to rebellion. Challenging our traditions and conventions, our entire way of life, was a first step toward recovering the moral authority we had lost to our hypocrisies.

———————

THE 1960S MADE DISSOCIATION from traditional America the very essence of a new American obsession: "authenticity." Suddenly, here in the United States, the freest society in the world, the idea of being "authentic" began to bloom in new ways. What did "authenticity" mean? It meant the embrace of new idealisms and new identities that explicitly untethered you from America's notorious hypocrisies. Authenticity was the great counterpoint to hypocrisy. It always asserted a new and alluring innocence against the corruptions of the old hypocrisies. The hippie identity of "peace and love" insisted on a new American way of life free of militarism, materialism, racism, sexism, and so on. Hippies strove to be innocent precisely in all those places where America was guilty. Radical antiwar activists— Students for a Democratic Society (SDS)—were innocent of both militarism and imperialism. Black power advocates were innocent of the complicity with white racism that they ascribed to earlier generations of blacks. Their militancy was really a declaration of incorruptibility: no more selling out, no more "going along with the system." Peace Corps volunteers were innocent of American imperialism: they would develop the Third World rather than exploit it. War on Poverty workers were innocent of the old fatalism that "the poor will always be with us": they would empower the poor. And, of course, feminists were innocent of that 1950s feminine ideal in which women were mere helpmates.

The 1960s formula for authenticity (dissociation from America's old hypocrisies) gave America a new cultural idea: *that America's moral authority and legitimacy were linked to the actual rejection of traditional America as a fundamentally hypocritical society.* Thus, rebellion is what made you authentic and what opened the way for society to recover moral authority. Rebellion, "revolution," dissent, civil and uncivil disobedience, "dropping out," "speaking truth to power"— all this became the moral high ground in the 1960s. In the long run, it would generate a new, alternative American identity, not to mention a new American liberalism.

6

Characterological Evil

IGRADUATED FROM COLLEGE in that most "1960s" of
years, 1968. In that year America saw Lyndon Johnson's
surprising abdication of power; the assassinations of Martin
Luther King and Bobby Kennedy; yet more riots in black
inner cities across the country; the deepening morass of
Vietnam; the radicalization of white middle-class peaceniks
into antiwar terrorists (such as the Weathermen); the bra-
zen occupation of university offices; the bombing of public
buildings; an unfolding feminist militancy; the emergence
of hippies (and their famous gathering at Woodstock); the
full-on embrace of "sexual liberation"; anarchistic movements, like the "Yippies" at the 1968 Democratic National
Convention in Chicago; the first stirrings of gay liberation;

and the deepening of black alienation into an ever more strident black nationalism.

For America, 1968 was a year of astringent transparency in which the entire culture became starkly visible through the gloss of hypocrisy. Our classic values around work and honor and allegiance to God and nation, our sense of a common culture unified by a common Judeo-Christian moral sensibility, our ability to assign the same meaning to events (Vietnam was suddenly imperialism to some and a patriotic stand against communism to others), our common national understanding of what our personal and public responsibilities should be—all this seemed to come apart in 1968 for lack of legitimate authority.

Has there ever been a single year in all of American history in which the American way of life came so thoroughly under siege? It was hard for anyone to go into that year and come out the same person. The young, especially, felt called upon to reinvent themselves, to experiment and explore their way into a more authentic life.

AND IT WAS IN THE SPIRIT OF THAT YEAR that I decided to take a trip to Africa—by way of Algeria. Africa had become a hugely important symbol for the new black pride movement in America. Prior to the mid-sixties, most blacks had given short shrift to our African past, seeing it as something remote and irrelevant, if not downright embarrassing. We knew very little about Africa. Our great urgency had been to overcome the discrimination that kept us from fully joining the modern world that we found ourselves in.

Moreover, the specter of Africa had been embarrassing to blacks because it fed into the idea that race was a strict determinism—that race was destiny. Put bluntly, it suggested that the "inferiority" that defined African blacks in American popular culture (Tarzan movies, etc.) also defined American blacks. The racial imagery of Africa argued for white supremacy, not against it.

Thus black nationalism's embrace of black Africa in the 1960s was both a defiant and psychologically revolutionary move in black America. It idealized Africa (just as Marcus Garvey's "Back to Africa" movement had done in the 1920s) into a black "golden age"—a fantasy territory where blacks had once lived idyllically as masters of their own fate and at one with God and nature. And from this Africa/Eden, blacks had been abducted into bondage by evil whites. But black nationalism was also, in its way, a legitimate psychic recovery effort. It sought to transform a mark of shame into a symbol of pride. It gave back to blacks their own history as one of the world's great stories—a journey narrative in which blacks were stolen out of an ancient black unity and cast into a terrible diaspora by the slave trade and then, after much suffering and overcoming, finally delivered to a new unity in the modern world.

Black nationalism in the 1960s pretended to be that new unity. "Blackness" (a word unheard of before the mid-sixties) was a vision of racial wholeness. It was an atavistic vision in which we blacks were connected by blood to that long-ago black unity, and now we would be restored to it in the modern world. This nationalism was primarily a redemption fantasy; it was a balm against the diminishment and suffering that American racism had actually subjected us to. It was a compensatory mythology that made us a little bigger than life to counterbalance all the denigration we had endured. Unfortunately, its gaze was always backward; it pined for a unity like we had supposedly known in our long-ago golden age—that time before the white man, before our fall. So just as America was finally opening real opportunities to us (university educations, entrée to corporate employment, the chance to run for political office), black nationalism was offering only the empty consolation of racial grandiosity, a kind of black supremacy. It had no idea how to guide us toward success in a modern society that was capitalistic and intensely competitive. To its credit, it wanted blackness to be a source of pride, but it had no real social capital to offer, no hard utilitarian knowledge of how we might achieve the concrete success in the actual world that would give substance to pride.

IF I FELLOW-TRAVELED FOR A WHILE with black national-ism, I was never a true believer. In the summer of 1970, when I had finally saved enough money from working in a poverty program to travel to Africa, I did not think I was "going home," or returning to the "motherland." I had read a little African literature by that time and had come across Léopold Sédar Senghor's concept of "negritude." (Senghor was the president of Senegal and a poet of considerable tal-ent.) But I couldn't buy "negritude" any more than I could buy "blackness." I have always believed that any attempt to turn race into politics, to seek power through race, is the beginning of evil. And who could know this better than a black American? So I was not drawn to Africa by any romance of "return." I wanted to see it for another reason. And this reason had much more to do with America than with Africa.

The compounding of American hypocrisies that oc-curred in the sixties—that great amassing of shames—brought forth a new and transformative "poetic truth" about America, a truth that had been only an indiscernible whisper before that decade. If this truth had been uttered here and there by the odd disgruntled voice, it had certainly never before the 1960s become established as a conventional truth for millions of Americans. This was the kind of "truth" that was hard to explicitly name, yet it profoundly transformed America—our culture as much as or more than our politics. Ultimately, it affected almost every area of public and private life. It generated a new "countercultural" American identity that would quickly evolve into a new form of cultural and political liberalism that, in turn, would send the country into decades of cultural warfare.

What is this "truth"? It begins in the assertion that America's indulgence in so many hypocrisies was not merely an anomaly. America wasn't a good and fair nation that only gave into hypocrisy here and there, now and then. No, this new "truth" was simply that America was innately—even characterologically—evil. In other words, the will to use evil as a means to power and wealth for a prosperous white (and largely male) elite was America's true raison d'être. Despite the founding fathers' fine talk of democracy, equality, and individual freedom, America's actual development was accompanied—and sometimes facilitated—by the practice of many evils: the relentless dehumanization of blacks, the relegation of women to a voteless second-class status, the conquering of the western frontier by tactics that were sometimes genocidal toward the Indians, the pillaging of natural resources, and so on. It could look as though democracy, in the minds of the founding fathers, was a concept of government only for the elite, thus leaving all others to endure the same abuses of power that democracy was conceived to overcome.

By actual example, many of these inarguably great men seemed as devoted to the abuses of power they fought against as to the freedom they fought for. There was, for example, Thomas Jefferson, who wrote words as timeless as any in the Bible—*"All men are created equal, . . . they are endowed by their Creator with certain unalienable rights."* Yet even in deep old age, Jefferson did not free the slave children he fathered, or the slave woman who bore them. Couldn't he have discreetly arranged to set his own progeny free? (Two of his four children by the slave Sally Hemings had managed to escape to freedom.) So here was a son of the American Revolution, not to mention the author of arguably the greatest articulation of freedom ever written, the Declaration of Independence, choosing to preserve the imperial prerogatives of his slave-owning caste over the freedom of his own children.

In the 1960s, the vision of America as an inherently evil society became the "poetic truth" of the new counterculture generation—this despite the launch of the Great Society, the War on Poverty, school busing for integration, affirmative action, the expansion of welfare, and so on. It became a kind of broad impressionism that determined the "authenticity" of people within that generation. The specter of American evil invited extremism as a "rational" response. If you arranged your beliefs, commitments, and even friendships around the poetic truth of American evil, then you were authentic. To the extent that you denied American evil—thus rejecting the poetic truth of that generation—you effectively aligned yourself with that evil. So the poetic truth of American evil was a radicalizing "truth." It literally made anti-Americanism a precondition for the nation's redemption from its past. Thus the spectacle in the late 1960s of upper-middle-class white kids trying to blow up public buildings inside their own country, and of the pseudo-Marxist Black Panthers provoking shootouts with the "pigs." This was the "truth" that gave us an increasingly militant and confrontational antiwar movement (including Kent State)—a movement not only against the war but also against that evil in the American character that caused the war. It gave us the counterculture itself. And ultimately, this "truth" gave the nation a broad, guilt-driven, moralistic liberalism in which at least a vague anti-Americanism was decency itself.

WHEN MY WIFE AND I BOARDED the plane at John F. Kennedy International Airport in the summer of 1970, headed to Africa, I was at the very least mildly intrigued with the idea that a current of evil ran through the American character. After all, I had lived with the evil of racism all my life, and I understood that evil, in some form, would always be with us. But I had never thought of the country as essentially evil—as if God had given evil to America as its special mission. Moreover, my parents—lifelong civil rights activists—had raised me to think of America not as a racist country but as a truly great country that was bedeviled by the human backwardness of racism. They thought of racism as a vestigial impulse from man's unevolved past that kept insinuating itself into the modern world.

So in fighting against racism, I had never been fighting against America; I had been fighting against racism in America.

But by the late 1960s, after the nation's habits of evil had been toted up and distilled into a holistic characterization of America as evil, the context of reform changed dramatically. In 1964 (the year the Civil Rights Act passed), the thought was that reformers were still fighting against the specific evils that plagued an otherwise admirable America—the disenfranchisement of black voters, the denial of equal opportunity to women, the militarism of Vietnam, and the like. But by 1968, for many, these specific evils were no longer seen as aberrations of the American character, but rather, as reflections of it. They pointed to its central truth. And if America was in fact characterologically evil, then there was no legitimate authority for reformers to negotiate with in the first place. How can you reform a society away from its evils when that society is inherently evil?

This broad characterization of America as inherently evil is what radicalized dissent in America. By my junior year in college—1967—I was no longer interested in fighting for school integration or fair housing laws. These suddenly seemed pedestrian in the context of America's characterological evil. And in those years, this presumption of intrinsic evil emerged as a defining theme for my generation. It was a vision of America that distinguished us from previous generations. We were different—and by implication morally superior—because we were the first generation daring enough to acknowledge our country's evil. So, paradoxically, we were enlarged by this evil. It gave my generation a sense of destiny, a job to do in history: to transform America away from its inherent evil.

The irony, of course, was that without this evil, the children of the 1960s had no special destiny; we were only ordinary. We spawned a liberalism that made this evil characterological—a poetic truth immune to all the actual truth that contradicted it. As such, America's evil would always provide us with a sense of purpose and destiny and even moral superiority.

It would also inspire—and justify—many forms of radicalism, from the political to the personal. After all, the greater the scope of American evil, the more we were called to radicalism. We couldn't reform our way past this evil; we had to assault it radically. And for many in my generation, radicalism became a high calling. It was integrity itself.

7

"The Battle of Algiers"

I SUPPOSE I WAS RATHER INFATUATED with radicalism in 1970 when my wife and I—she twenty-one and Jewish; me twenty-three and black—arrived in Algiers, Algeria, on the first stop of our African trip. To say that we were naïve would be extreme understatement—an American black and an American Jew turning up in bellbottom jeans and a miniskirt (so cool back in the states) in a Muslim country. And yet we were determined to be intrepid, to fully experience this surprisingly beautiful city that sloped down from high sunny hills to the languid Mediterranean. This city, along with Oran, Algeria, was the literary territory of Albert Camus. It was also the romantic backdrop that had given a certain revolutionary chic to the film *The Battle of*

Algiers—an iconic film for my generation in which radical-ism and even terrorism were the underdogs one rooted for.

In fact, this entire trip to Africa was organized around visits to cities like Algiers, cities associated with the independence movements and the revolutions that had swept across the Third World in the 1950s and 1960s. The idea was to visit "new societies" that had won independence from Western imperialism and were now determined to reinvent themselves outside the old colonial framework. When you defeated Western evil and created a new society absent that evil, the claim was that you created morally evolved human beings—a "new man," as it were, innocent of all the old Western evils. I wanted to see if there was anything to this. In other words, was there something new under the sun, some counterpoint to the American way of life that was better? I was skeptical, but at twenty-three, I needed to see the world a little for myself.

BUT THE MEN WE SAW in the first two days of walking the city of Algiers hardly seemed "new." And indeed, there were men everywhere. It seemed to be a city of men, with women consigned to the periphery of public spaces. My poor wife was gawked at even when she wore baggy jeans, a raincoat, and a headscarf. Everywhere little clusters of men stood around aimlessly—and a little lasciviously—in the middle of the day. There was no bustle to the city. Restaurants were a little confounded by the prospect of tourists. They wanted our business, but they weren't sure how to feed us, and they seemed a little embarrassed to offer us the local fare. I quickly realized that we were the only guests at the famous Algiers Hotel, where Churchill and Eisenhower had planned the Allied invasion in 1943. It was a proud hotel, but now caught in the paradox of selling itself as an oasis of colonial grandeur in a revolutionary country. There were few cabs at its entrance, and if you went with one, the driver trailed you around all day hoping to catch you again.

When Algiers had been part of France, it had been a vital and storied city—the largest city in France next to Paris. Yet, for all its beauty, the native Arab population had been treated much like blacks had been treated in America. Now the French had been defeated and expelled, the revolution had been achieved, and yet the city seemed both listless and tense.

It was on our second afternoon in the city, while walking up a street in central Algiers and feeling depressed about our decision to spend a full week here, that we ran into the American Black Panthers. A voice called out from a passing car. "Hey, brother!" It was unmistakably a black American inflection, and jarring to hear in downtown Algiers. Then I saw him, his head sticking out the of driver's window, a huge American-style afro very much like my own, and that giddy excitement on his face that comes over people when they spot a kinsman—a "brother"—completely out of context, thousands of miles from home, and in a place where one had lost all hope of such an encounter. I later learned that there was more to his excitement than simple surprise. There was also the loneliness of exile, and the peculiar neediness it breeds in people who would otherwise never give in to neediness. He pulled his car wildly to the curb, jumped out, and, embarrassed by his own excitement, gave me a black-power handshake that literally hurt.

I knew that he was an American Black Panther the moment I'd heard the black American inflection in his voice. I knew that a contingent of Panthers—on the run from American authorities—had been given political asylum by the Algerian government. I knew that Eldridge Cleaver, the famous author of *Soul on Ice*, was their leader, but I never expected to actually meet any of them. I was curious, even hopeful that I might run into them, but I feared they would only see me as a kind of revolutionary tourist and not want to be bothered.

So I was shocked to see how desperate they were for my meager company. And, with every civility, they embraced my wife as if she was, at the very least, an honorary kinsman. The man who stopped us introduced himself as "DC." He flatly told us that he needed to talk, needed to hear what was going on back in the States. There were two other men (also Panthers) in his small car, but he insisted that we all pile in and go back to their "villa" and feast on the local shrimp, which he promised we would love. Within ten minutes we were seated in the beautifully appointed upstairs living room of the spacious villa that had been provided to the American Black Panthers by the Algerian government.

I was star-struck and thought Eldridge or Kathleen Cleaver might materialize at any moment. But apparently the Cleavers were in North Korea (another revolutionary safe haven) preparing for the birth of a child. DC was an enthusiastic and engaging host and we had a great time. The shrimp—a little like Louisiana crawfish—were delicious, and I did my best to update him on the current scene back home.

But the most striking thing about DC was his homesickness. He spoke rapturously of his years in the San Francisco Bay Area, and it was surprising to realize that he envied my wife and me for our ability simply to go to the airport and fly home if we wanted to—for the fact that we were still on the right side of the law in America. I had thought naïvely that he was the man at the fascinating center of things—that he was likely making history, while I was just a tourist. But he said nothing about Algiers; it was all the Bay Area, how he'd come there as a teenager from a small town in Missouri, and how he'd come of age there.

When he became a little embarrassed by his homesickness, he would quickly revert to familiar Panther rhetoric—"we want complete radical change," we want to "mash and destroy the capitalist system," and so on. In these rhetorical disquisitions, he employed the word "revolution" as a kind of touchstone. The word had no clear meaning and no practical connection to the real world. (How would six or so men exiled in a villa in Algiers "mash and destroy the capitalist system"?) Yet the mere word seemed to center DC and restore his sense of authority. And he spoke it mantra-like, as if to will himself away from some swamp of feelings and back onto solid ground.

I remember feeling disappointed. Probably it was Eldridge Cleaver's fame as a daring and eloquent writer (*Soul on Ice* had bewitched young people all across America) that gave the Panthers a reputation as intellectual outlaws as well as gun-carrying revolutionaries. I guess I'd expected to see some of this when I met DC—some new fusion of revolutionary ideas culled from all the Third World revolutions of that era and applied to the American situation. Most of all, I wanted to know if there truly was no hope of reforming a country like America.

When I found the nerve to ask this question, DC became fatherly, as if he understood that part of his mission as a revolutionary was to bring along people like me. But then he only resorted to the old Panther chestnut of America as "Babylon"—Panther code for a nation lost to capitalist greed, imperialism, and all manner of attendant evils. "Babylon" was a categorical and characterological assessment of the American nation, and it was a complete dismissal. He spoke as if pained to bring me this truth: reform was not a realistic possibility for America.

At his invitation, we showed up the next day for lunch. There was more shrimp, more talk of home. DC was a genuinely likable man and—ironically—what he clearly enjoyed most about us was simply that we were Americans. But two other Panthers—the same two who had been in the car when he first picked us up—seemed now to be nervous of us. As the afternoon wore on, I noticed them moving around the periphery of the room, parting the closed curtains ever so slightly to peek out. A sliver of light would quickly enter the room and then fade. It was a sunny afternoon, but the closed curtains gave the room a wintry cast. They never looked us in the eye.

DC went on as amicably as ever, but I was suddenly struck with the obvious: how vulnerable we were in this house with these men on the run, guns no doubt just out of sight, and in a country that was openly hostile to America. On summer break in college I had driven a city bus up and down the long arteries of Chicago's South Side on the night shift. I had learned to trust certain instincts—to notice, for example, that the smiling teenager on his way home from a house party at 2:00 A.M. might not be what he appeared to be. I was robbed a few times; I was threatened many times. The veteran drivers taught us young summer replacements to look closely at people and to "breeze" past a bus stop that didn't feel right. "There's no honor in dying to drive a bus," they would say.

So in the Black Panthers' villa in the center of Algiers, a world away from Chicago, I suddenly knew that I was simply in the company of thugs. I saw that their eyes were a little dead. It occurred to me that they could kill, or already had. Only DC, obviously in charge while the Cleavers were gone, and driven by homesickness, was even interested in conversation. The others laughed here and there but never said much.

Then someone said "the French teacher" (provided by the Algerian government) was about to arrive. I saw my chance. I grabbed my wife's hand and said we would never want to interrupt their French lesson. We would take a walk and see them later on. DC smiled apologetically, making it clear that he would much rather keep talking than take a French lesson.

On the street, walking fast, we found a cab, took it to the hotel, and asked the driver to wait. We then packed our bags, checked out, and took the cab straight to the airport, though we were not scheduled to leave Algiers for four more days. My wife was a little confused. Was it really necessary to rush like this? It was a balmy sunny afternoon. The

Mediterranean was blue and lovely. We would talk much about this later, but then all I could say was that I was not a revolutionary and that we were going to "breeze" this stop.

AT THE AIRPORT, a young black American woman material-ized out of nowhere to ask if she could be of help. "I speak French," she said. At first I felt like DC must have felt when he spotted me, an American "brother," walking down the street in a foreign city. I had the feeling that I knew her, that she might have grown up in my neighborhood. With amazing efficiency, she rearranged our flight schedule to get us out of Algiers on a flight that night to our next stop, Lagos, Nigeria. Yet she was so clearly outside any recogniz-able context—she was not a tourist or an exchange student or a businesswoman—that I knew right away she had to be CIA. (I later heard from several people that the Central Intelligence Agency had a small contingent in Algiers to watch the comings and goings of the Panthers, who were, after all, international fugitives—people charged back home with murder and plane hijacking.)

At the time, what shocked me most about this con-jecture was that it comforted me. It meant that America knew where we were. Pretending only to make friendly chatter, she interviewed us as she redid our travel plans:

what brought us to Algiers, did we know people here; what college had we gone to, and so on. I told her only that we had run into some Americans and had a good time, but now we were ready to go. It was the oddest conversation. I knew who she was and she knew that I knew. I also then suspected that we had been watched in Algiers and that she knew more about me than she was saying. Yet none of this was acknowledged. Still, somehow there was a communication, and we seemed finally to strike a note of good faith. I think she simply concluded that we were in fact the fools that we appeared to be.

8

No Past,
No Future

Later, back home in the States, I learned that the man we knew as DC had achieved a quick moment of fame before disappearing into exile. In 1970, Leonard Bernstein, the great Broadway composer, had held a fundraiser for the New York Black Panthers in his opulent Park Avenue apartment. The social critic and "new journalist" Tom Wolfe made this party the stuff of legend by writing about it, first in *New York* magazine and then in his famous book *Radical Chic & Mau Mauing the Flake Catchers*. Here on indelible display was the pretentiousness, self-congratulation, and self-effacing political correctness of wealthy whites seeking a kind of moral authenticity through mere proximity to "angry blacks." Wolfe's description of this party was far ahead of its time as a portrait of white guilt.

DC had been the Panther spokesman at the event. When Bernstein asked him what "tactics" he would use to achieve his goals, DC said, according to the *New York Times*, "If business won't give us full employment, then we must take the means of production and put them in the hands of the people." Bernstein replied with that ingratiating white-boy hipness that makes people cringe, "I dig absolutely"—thereby effectively endorsing a Marxist revolution from his Park Avenue apartment if blacks did not get full employment.

Not long after the Bernstein party, DC was charged with the murder of one Eugene Anderson, a Panther who had been a police informant in Baltimore. DC claimed that he had nothing to do with the crime. Yet, after a warrant for his arrest was issued, he fled to Algiers, where, in due course, he hailed me down on the street. I knew nothing of the charges against him at the time.

While we actually spent many hours in easy and frank conversation, I knew DC only briefly. I liked him. He was a recognizable type to me—a goodhearted "country" black enthralled by the sophistication of the Bay Area when he had moved there as a teenager from rural Missouri. Yet he had a restless intelligence and a newfound racial pride that drove him to want more than his background had prepared him for. It was a common story in the late 1960s. We blacks were emerging from segregation and facing a future of considerable possibility, yet the deprivations of segregation had left many of us without the necessary social capital and know-how to exploit those possibilities. This was the circumstance that turned our hard-won freedom into a harsh mistress. Freedom would strip us of excuses for our shortcomings; it would point only to our inadequacies (with no real regard for the oppression that caused them) and give the impression that the stereotype of black "inferiority" was in fact true.

I understood little of this at the time. But I could see that DC had no clear place in the world. He did not have the formal education to move into a bright American future, even though that possibility was, by then, opening up everywhere back home. So he would be a black revolutionary and thus a little larger than life (he was the Panther "field marshal" in charge of weapons and security). Caught between a past that had deprived him and a future that he couldn't seize, he chose the outlaw's grandiosity.

Perhaps this was the profile of most Panthers. Perhaps they comprised a little society of men and women who had no place in the past or in the future, and so had invented a world of "revolution" that might give them a sense of place and importance. In this invented world they would not be "nowhere people" holed up in a Third World backwater; they would be "field marshals" or "ministers" of this or that.

(Eldridge Cleaver was the minister of information.) Everyone would have a paramilitary title—in effect a designation of place within the revolution as though revolution were an actual country they were defending.

─────────────

BUT THIS PROBLEM OF PLACELESSNESS was hardly limited to the Panthers. Formerly oppressed people around the world in the 1950s and 1960s were emerging from oppression and trying to find their way into a new future of greater self-determination, but also a future that their very oppression had ill-equipped them for. All across sub-Saharan Africa, Asia, and South America, the glory of hard-won independence was soon followed by the violence and chaos of religious, ethnic, and ideological factionalism. It was almost formulaic: independence, a quick lull in which high hopes prevailed, and then years, if not decades, of civil war, strongmen dictators, atrocities, and coups.

One reason for this is that the formerly oppressed—with no way back to the golden past and no easy way ahead—almost reflexively invent new group identities to give themselves structure, a sense of place, and a platform upon which to pursue power. It was *after* the passage of the 1964 Civil Rights Act and the 1965 Voting Rights Act—legislation meant to finally and truly emancipate blacks—that we black

Americans invented "blackness" as a new identity. Having at last won the freedom to function as individuals, we went straight to group identity to take us forward. "Black unity" would deliver us.

But of course this only tries to make a magic out of being black, as if racial self-love and solidarity were the same thing as individual will and character—as if "black pride" could do the individual's hard work of developing into a person who can compete successfully in the modern world. Black culture is a tremendous resource for the individual. But culture is vastly different from the shallow iconography of the "blackness" identity. This identity skims over the fundamental human reality expressed so well in Ralph Ellison's novel *Invisible Man*. A fictional college professor, alluding to James Joyce's character Stephen Daedalus, says, "Stephen's problem, like ours [the formerly oppressed], was not actually one of creating the uncreated conscience of [our] race, but of creating the *uncreated features of [our] face*. Our task is that of making ourselves individuals. The conscience of a race is the gift of its individuals who see, evaluate, record . . ." And, I would add, *not the other way around*. Individuals, out of a complex mix of motivations (race probably least among them), pursue their dreams and passions, and then, inevitably, the group blossoms.

But when there is a strong sense of placelessness within the group, when both the past and the future seem impossible—

as was the case for so many newly liberated people in the late 1960s—those just moving out of oppression often ask their group identity to stand in for their individual identity. That is, they invent a grandiose idea of the group that gives them self-esteem despite the fact that they lack the resources and the knowledge to go forward as individuals. Here group identity has little to do with a rich cultural past (of which they may be entirely ignorant); its real purpose is to impart self-esteem to people who live in a new freedom they are unprepared to capitalize on. "Black pride," "black power," and "blackness" cover over the confusion and shortcomings of the black individual who is suddenly free but without a compass. It assuages those for whom the fruits of freedom suddenly hang low but nevertheless still out of reach.

Group identities that compensate for the deprived background of the individual with a grandiose vision of the group always bring forward into new freedom the "poetic truth" that the group's former oppressor, its old nemesis, is still alive and well. These identities always claim that the oppressor's evil was an entrenched feature of character rather than a lapse of character. And once the evil is characterological, it is "poetic" and eternal; it is truer than all facts to the contrary. "Neocolonialism," "structural racism," "male bias," and "environmental indifference" are all terms that "poeticize" America's old evils. And once "poeticized," they become givens in our conversation. They are reality no matter what the reality actually is. Thus, even in freedom, those who were victimized remain victimized even as most Americans have forsworn any desire to victimize. These identities declare that greater freedom is no harbor from victimization.

As the formerly oppressed move into greater and greater freedom, they are often more wedded to the idea of themselves as oppressed than to the reality that they are freer than ever. Their grievance against their former oppressor is leverage, entitlement, and even self-esteem within the larger society. It is power. And in that placelessness that comes with new freedom, grievance becomes a kind of "place." After our civil rights victories in the mid-1960s, we black Americans found a recognizable home in grievance. Here we knew ourselves and felt empowered. Here was "place" amid the terrors of new freedom.

The problem is that this "place" is in the past. And it does no good to adapt to a past that is only an echo now. There is no refuge there. We have been called upon to step into the modern world despite our anxieties. Our mistake has been to make the poetic truth of America's intractable racism into a "place"—a strategy that only keeps us victims even when the world, hesitantly or not, invites us to live as free men and women.

9

America's
"Characterological Evil"

A Pillar of Identity

WHEN I TRAVELED TO AFRICA back in 1970, it was partly because I had been more and more seduced by this great looming idea of America's characterological evil. It was such a summary judgment, and, at the time, still new and audacious. It had not existed in the original civil rights movement of the 1950s and early 1960s. Martin Luther King Jr. had never charged America with an inherent and intractable evil. He had lived in good faith with America, believing in reform and the innate goodwill of the American character, even as he also lived under constant threat of assassination. Still, when his assassination actually came to pass—with an almost macabre predictability—young blacks, like myself (and many whites as well), saw it as a final straw. The evil character of America would always prevail over decency.

I came of age—in my early twenties—precisely when this idea began to take hold. Suddenly it was everywhere among the young. Belief in America's evil was the new faith that launched you into a sophistication that your parents could never understand. And in linking you to the disaffection of your generation, it made youth itself into a *group* identity that bore witness to the nation's evil and that, simultaneously, embraced a new "counterculture" innocence. Coming out of this identity, you owed nothing to your parent's conventional expectations for your life. You could go to medical or law school if you wanted, but you could also roll in the mud at Woodstock, do drugs, or join a commune.

A result of this generation's explicit knowledge of America's historical evils was to make social and political morality a more important measure of character than private morality. In the 1950s, your private morality was the measure of your character; in the 1960s, your stance against war, racism, and sexism became far more important measures—so important that you were granted considerable license in the private realm. Sleep with whomever you wanted, explore your sexuality, expand your mind with whatever drug you liked, forgo marriage, follow your instincts and impulses as inner truths, enjoy hedonism as a kind of radical authenticity. The only important thing was that you were dissociated from American evil. Dissociation from this evil became a pillar of identity for my generation.

But I was from the working class. I had put myself through college. I couldn't afford to bank my life on the dramatic notion that America was characterologically evil unless it was actually true. Africa was a continent full of new countries that had banked their fate on precisely this view of their former oppressors. I wanted to see some of these countries then led by a generation of charismatic men who had won hard-fought revolutions against their Western oppressors—Jomo Kenyatta of Kenya, Kwame Nkrumah of Ghana, and Léopold Sédar Senghor of Senegal. They were all seen as redeemers—the selfless founding fathers of newly independent nations. And, having thrown off the yoke of colonialism, there was the expectation that their countries would begin to flourish.

But in fact they were not flourishing. We left Algeria in the middle of the night and landed the next morning on the other side of the Sahara Desert in Lagos, Nigeria, where we—along with all the passengers on our flight—were held at gunpoint in the airport for several hours for mysterious reasons having to do with the Biafran War. Finally, we made it to Nkrumah's Ghana, which only looked more and more bedraggled and directionless—a sharp contrast to the revolutionary glory that Kwame Nkrumah had projected around the world. (Kwame was fast becoming a popular name for male babies among black Americans.) Food was scarce and unrelievedly bad even in the American hotel in the capital city of Accra. You saw chickens pecking for food in open sewers, and then at dinner you wondered at the gray meat on your plate smothered in nondescript brown gravy. Then there were ten days in Dakar, Senegal, where Senghor, the father of "negritude," was president. But it wasn't "negritude" that made Dakar a little more bearable than Accra. There were still some French there, and it was their fast-fading idea of Dakar as an African Paris that meant better food and the hint of a café society.

The Africa we saw was, at best, adrift. The Africans themselves—as opposed to the Middle Eastern and European shopkeepers and middlemen—looked a little abandoned. Today I would say they were stuck in placelessness. They obviously didn't want to go back to their colonial past, yet, except for a small, educated elite, they had no clear idea of how to move into the future. They had wanted self-determination, but they had not been acculturated to modernity. How does one do self-determination without fully understanding the demands of the modern world?

In Dakar, an enterprising middle-aged man—someone who would surely have owned his own business had he been born in America—appeared every day outside our hotel trying to sell us the same malformed and unfinished wooden sculpture. Every day a different story and a different price attached to this "sculpture." The man was charming and quick, but I also sensed an anger and impatience just beneath the surface. He scared me a little. One morning, out of sheer frustration, I gave him five dollars (a lot of money then), but then walked away without taking the sculpture. Within a minute, I felt a tug on my sleeve. Angrily, he pushed the money and the ugly little sculpture back into my hands—as if to be rid of not only me but also a part of himself he couldn't stand. Then he stormed off. I had hurt his pride, and I felt terrible. I chased him down, gave him the money again, and took the sculpture (which I have to this day). His umbrage was still visible, but he accepted the deal.

In 1970, I had no way of understanding an encounter like this. Now a few things are clear. I was conspicuously American. My voluminous Afro only drove that point home. Thus I was an emissary from modernity itself. When I gave him money without taking his sculpture, I didn't just devalue him and his culture; I virtually mocked his historical circumstance by reminding him of what he already knew: that he was outside of history, that he was not of the modern world and had nothing really to offer me that I wanted or needed. Yes, the world by then knew that African art could be world-class. Picasso, among others, had brought its genius to the West. But he would not have known about Picasso, or even much about the art of woodcarving within his own culture. He wanted to be a tradesman, a businessman. But his ignorance even of what he was selling sabotaged his entrepreneurialism. So when I gave him money but rejected his statue, I treated him like a beggar to whom one gives alms, not like a businessman.

And wouldn't a man like this—and the millions like him all across Africa, the Middle East, and the Third World generally—soon be in need of a politics to fight back with. Wouldn't he need a political identity that lessened the sting of his individual humiliation by making him a member of an aggrieved collective. Wouldn't some ideology or other—nationalism, cultural nationalism, pan-Africanism, some version of Marxism, negritude, Islamism, jihadism, any idea of "unity" that merges the individual with the group—come into play to console individual alienation by normalizing it, by making it a collective rather than individual experience. Your humiliation does not reflect on you. You languish outside of history—hawking shapeless pieces of ebony on the streets of Dakar—because you belong to a people who were pushed out of history and exploited, first by colonialism and then by neocolonialism.

Placelessness literally demands a political identity that collectivizes people, one that herds them into victim-focused identities and consoles them with a vague myth of their own human superiority. Léopold Senghor, the first president of newly independent Senegal and the father of "negritude," said, "Far from seeing in one's blackness inferiority, one accepts it; one lays claim to it with pride; one cultivates it lovingly." Marcus Garvey, a popular racialist black American leader in the 1920s, said, "Negroes, teach your children that they are the direct descendants of the greatest and proudest race who ever peopled the earth." The Islamic extremism that so threatens the world today operates by the same formula: devout followers of Allah are superior to their decadent former oppressors (mere infidels) in the West. The feminism that came out of the 1960s argued that if women were victimized by male chauvinism, they were also superior to men in vital ways. ("If women ruled the world there would be no wars" was a feminist mantra in the 1970s.)

All these identities assign a "place" against the experience of placelessness by giving the formerly oppressed an idea both of their victimization and their superiority. This "places" them back into the world and into the flow of history. You are somebody, these identities say. You were simply overwhelmed by your oppressor's determination to exploit you. Thus the consoling irony at the heart of victimization: you possess an inherent human supremacy to those who humiliated you.

———————————

BUT THERE IS A PRICE for this consolation: all these victim-focused identities are premised on a belief in the character-ological evil of America and the entire white Western world. This broad assumption is the idea that makes them work, that makes for that sweet concoction of victimization and superiority. So the very people who were freed by America's (and the West's) acknowledgment of its past wrongs then made that acknowledgment into a poetic truth that they could build their identities in reaction to. Once America's evil became "poetic" (permanently true), the formerly oppressed could make victimization an ongoing feature of their identity—despite the fact that their actual victimiza-tion had greatly declined.

And think of all the millions of people across the world who can find not only consolation in such an identity but also self-esteem, actual entitlements, and real political power—and not just the poor and dark-skinned people of the world but also the Park Avenue feminist, the black affirmative-action baby from a well-heeled background, and white liberals generally who seek power through an identifi-cation with America's victims. Today, all these identities are leverage in a culture contrite over its past.

The point is that these identities—driven by the need for "place," esteem, and power—keep the idea of American/Western characterological evil alive as an axiomatic truth in the modern world, as much a given as the weather. In other words, this charge of evil against the white West is one of the largest and most influential ideas of our age—and this despite the dramatic retreat of America and the West from these evils. The scope and power of this idea—its enormous influence in the world—is not a measure of its truth or accuracy; it is a measure of the great neediness in the world for such an idea, for an idea that lets the formerly oppressed defend their esteem, on the one hand, and pursue power in the name of their past victimization, on the other. It is also an idea that gave a contrite white America (and Western world) a new and essentially repentant liberalism.

In this striking vision of the white Western world as characterologically evil, both the former dark-skinned victims of this evil and its former white perpetrators found a common idea out of which to negotiate a future. This vision restored esteem to the victims (simply by acknowledging that they were victims rather than inferiors) and gave them a means to power; likewise, it opened a road to redemption and power for the former white perpetrators. This notion of America's characterological evil became the basis of a new social contract in America.

10

The Denouement

NOT MUCH OF THIS WAS CLEAR to me in 1970 as we traveled through Africa. But one thing did become clearer as the trip progressed. Back home, I had been flirting with real radicalism—not radicalism to the point of violence, but radicalism nonetheless. For me that meant living a life that would presume America's evil and that would be forever disdainful toward and subversive of traditional America. It meant I would be a radical liberal living in bad faith with my country—"in it but not of it," as we used to say back then. So here in my early twenties I genuinely wondered if the subversive life wasn't the only truly honorable life. Wouldn't it be "selling out" (the cardinal sin of the counterculture) to look past America's evil and cast my fate in the mainstream?

On some level I knew, even at the time, that the trip to Africa was an attempt to resolve this dilemma. I wanted to see real radicalism in the faces of people in a society where it had actually come to hold sway. I wanted to see what it looked like as a governing reality in a real society. And this is pretty much what I accomplished on that trip. I didn't understand placelessness at the time, or the pursuit of esteem through grandiose identities. But, beginning with our encounter with the Black Panthers in Algiers, I knew that I was seeing what I needed to see. And I began to feel a growing certainty within myself. My dilemma was resolving itself. The more we traveled—a month and a half in all—the firmer my certainty became. And when we at last boarded the plane in Dakar headed for New York, I felt at peace. I was clear. The American mainstream would be my fate.

———————

THE CLARITY I FOUND ON THAT TRIP was based on one realization: I learned that America, for all its faults and failings, was not intractably evil. In the Black Panther villa in Algiers, on those balmy afternoons eating the local shrimp, I spent time with people who had banked their entire lives on America's inherent evil—and on the inherent evil of capitalism. On one level, they were glamorous figures, revolutionaries ensconced in a lavish villa provided by the new radical government of Algeria. The impression was of a new and more perfect world order just around the corner, and these special people with the moral imagination to see it coming would soon be marching in victory.

Yet I could see that as human beings they were homesick and in despair. As revolutionaries, they were impotent and hopelessly lost. It was like seeing a pretty woman whose smile unfolds to reveal teeth black with rot. They had no future whatsoever, and so they were chilling to behold. We had all grown up in segregation. We all had war stories. And we all had legitimate beefs against America. But to embrace the idea that America and capitalism were permanent oppressors was self-destructive and indulgent. It cut us off from both the past and the future. It left us in the cul-de-sac of placelessness, though I could not have described it this way at the time. But I could see even then that someone like DC had gotten himself into the same cul-de-sac as the street hawker selling chunks of wood as art in Dakar. They were both languishing in a truly existential circumstance. And they were both consoled by a faith in the evil of America and the West.

Looking back, I now think of DC as a cautionary tale, an essentially softhearted man who had allowed himself to be captured by a bad idea—that his country was irretrievably evil. Unlike most other Black Panthers, he ended up living a long—if strained—life. Soon after I met him, the

Algerian government began to tire of supporting the Black Panthers in their fast-fading glory while so many Algerians languished in poverty. At the end of July 1972, another American black, George Wright, along with four other men and women, hijacked a plane in America en route to Miami and then extorted a $1 million ransom from the Federal Bureau of Investigation. The hijackers ordered the pilots to take them to Boston and then Algeria. Eldridge Cleaver wanted the money and wrote an open letter to Houari Boumediene, the president of Algeria, in effect asking the government to continue supporting the cause of black American liberation. But the Algerian government recovered the ransom money and returned it to American authorities. Algeria's romance with black American revolutionaries was over.

DC, who by then had made hay of his French lessons, made his way to France, where he lived for the rest of his life in exile from America and the San Francisco Bay Area that he so loved. Wanted always by the FBI, he lived an underground life even in France. He worked as a house painter in Paris and did other odd jobs. He ended up in Camps-sur-l'Agly, France, where, at the age of seventy-four, after a day spent working in his garden, he apparently died in his sleep.

I was lucky. After one of my radical kitchen-table rants against America toward the end of the 1960s, my father—

the son of a man born in slavery—had said to me: "You know, you shouldn't underestimate America. This is a strong country." I protested, started in on racism once again. He said, "No, it's strong enough to change. You can't imagine the amount of change I've seen in my own lifetime."

11

After Evil, "The Good"

WHEN A SOCIETY ACKNOWLEDGES that evil has been an element of its character, an easy logic follows: not only must that society redeem itself, but it must do so through nothing less than an evolution of character. That is, redemption requires that the hearts and minds of people evolve past the old impulses to evil. Only this sort of moral evolution, the logic argues, can transform the culture and the collective psychology of a society once it has confessed to evil. Only moral evolution truly deactivates the old evils, turns them into solemn and cautionary memories. Most importantly, this logic has it that only such profound evolution can restore legitimacy to government in a society living under the veil of its own confession.

But how does a society pursue such an evolution? By what means can a government revive its beleaguered legitimacy? Since the 1960s, America has had one overriding answer: to give America a new mission beyond freedom, to establish "The Good" as a national mission on a par with freedom. Freedom had always been America's great promise to itself and the world, and for many Americans this promise had been an actual reality. Yet this devotion to freedom had not stopped America from the evil of denying freedom to millions of its own citizens. So wasn't it self-evident that freedom needed help—that freedom alone would never again be enough to bring legitimacy to the government and the society?

Therefore, the 1960s gave us the idea that there could be no true freedom without a corresponding commitment to The Good. In fact, only by giving The Good at least a slight priority over freedom was it possible to realize the fruits of freedom. Jean-Paul Sartre in the 1940s famously said, "Existence precedes essence." The 1960s said, "The Good precedes freedom." Freedom is essentially only a condition, an absence of constraints and barriers; it is not in itself an agent of change. But The Good is such an agent; it is an activism. It wants to remake the world. And the 1960s had uncovered so much injustice and inequality (America's characterological evil) that The Good became utterly irresistible, even when it stepped on freedom. So freedom came out of the 1960s limping a little and morally tarnished, while The Good seemed to glow with promise.

What is The Good? Well, The Good that I am speaking of is not that timeless and hard-earned Good that our great religions and great secular documents (like the US Constitution) try to shepherd us toward. The Ten Commandments and the Bill of Rights spell out disciplines (moral and political) that, among other things, align us with The Good when we follow them ardently. This Good is earned the hard way by adhering to that long litany of classic human virtues—selflessness, courage, humility, sacrifice, fidelity, and so on. Think of those rare white southerners in the 1950s who stood up against segregation, or the black freedom riders in the early 1960s who walked peacefully into the very mouth of racial hatred and violence.

Here The Good is not the gift of public policy but rather of character. It is not a state of being that one achieves and then dwells in ever after, nor is it a badge that one gets to wear by merely subscribing to political correctness. What might be called The Real Good is what follows from moral responsibility—both personal and collective. And it is a struggle to know what moral responsibility calls for in a given situation. Thus The Real Good is never a finished thing, and we never get to sum ourselves up as good; rather, The Real Good is conscientiousness itself, an ongoing effort.

But in the 1960s, there was no patience for so demanding an idea. The new accusation of characterological evil suddenly threatened the legitimacy of both the government and the broader culture. America needed an idea of The Good that was untethered to character, or at least not dependent on much character. We needed to make The Good into something that was easy, something that could be waved about in the air like a white flag of surrender—something that would instantly disassociate us from the nation's evil past.

However, by relegating The Good to the government, and making it a matter of public policy, we transformed it from an earnest and personal moral struggle into a glib cultural symbolism. And as a mere symbolism, The Good became a brittle and thoughtless thing: Americans could navigate around any guilt over the past simply by acquiescing to governmental interventions—the War on Poverty, school busing, lenient welfare policies, affirmative action, and so on. This is how the American Left labored to win back moral authority and legitimacy after the 1960s—by allowing support for public policy to stand in as evidence of an evolution in private conscience.

So the actual purpose of The Good became *absolution* for the American people and the government, and not actual reform for minorities. The appeal of affirmative action was not the uplift of blacks and women, but the fact that support for such a policy was a shield against charges of racism and sexism. Virtually all these "good" reforms failed and mired us in all manner of unintended consequences. But their failures were beside the point. These policies were expressions of America's *regret* over its bigotries and sins. They weren't policies so much as apologias.

A corruption that came out of the 1960s was to reduce The Good to little more than apology for the past. Yet there was an irony: as apologies, these policies of The Good were effective in restoring a degree of moral legitimacy to what had been a clearly racist American democracy, this despite the fact that they caused much harm and achieved very little good.

12

The New Liberalism

T HE 1960S GAVE AMERICA a new political liberalism focused more on achieving The Good than on ensuring individual freedom. This was quite radical because it defied the classic Jeffersonian liberalism that had always made individual freedom its great goal. It was this classic liberalism that had enabled the early civil rights movement (pre-1964) to keep faith with America. But the new liberalism made The Good its lodestar.

This meant something very specific: that the new liberalism wanted America's classic ideals of justice, fairness, and equality—the American dream itself—to be contingent on an activism of The Good rather than on the disciplines of freedom. In other words, it put America's ideals, and the moral authority of the American society generally, into the hands, so to speak, of The Good. Conversely, it showed little faith that the self-restraints that real freedom depends on—fair competition by merit, individual initiative, and equality of opportunity rather than of result—would ever be enough to deliver us to our best ideals. Classic freedom-focused liberalism had been about process, about restraining the intrusive hand of the state, about guaranteeing individual rights and liberties. But the new post-1960s liberalism screamed that that process was not enough. Given that our democracy was in a crisis of legitimacy, we needed a proactive liberalism that could guarantee results, not simply refrain from discrimination.

America needed to combat the charge of characterological evil with *proof* of its characterological virtue. The nation's fundamental innocence had to be made self-evident. This was the cultural and political mandate that came out of the 1960s; and, because it was a mandate that our very legitimacy seemed to depend on, it opened a great vein of political power. Those who spoke and acted in its name carried the mantle of the nation's moral legitimacy. And this was their claim to power.

The new liberalism took on this mandate as its raison d'être, its creed, and thereby joined itself to this deep vein of power that went well beyond politics and into the realm of American culture itself. In fact this was, among other things, a mandate first of all to transform the culture (win the culture and the politics will follow). Thus post-1960s liberalism was devoted to "liberalizing" or "progressivizing" the culture in almost every area of life—from the mores surrounding marriage and family to the aesthetics of art, music, and literature to the standards of excellence in public education. Ultimately, this liberalism wanted to generate an altogether new American identity, one devoid of all hint of past hypocrisies and evils. It wanted to start America afresh in a new innocence.

To this end, it added two new overarching principles to its liberal version of the American identity: dissociation and relativism. These principles were meant to hold the American identity accountable to The Good—to the creation of a society cleansed of its old characterological evil. Unlike The Good, freedom is grounded in a kind of passivism and restraint, a long series of difficult "nots"—we will not discriminate, not interfere with free markets, not tell people what to say or believe, not overtax, and so on. I would argue that it was precisely the restraints of freedom, of classical liberalism, that finally expanded freedom for blacks and other minorities.

But dissociation and relativism gave the government and the American Left an opposite message: be activists, socially engineer The Good into existence. We trusted in the restraints of freedom, and where did that get us? The

War on Poverty and the Great Society were governmental activisms on behalf of The Good. They wouldn't wait for some "invisible hand" to lead America to full equality; they would engineer us into equality right away. If these principles stepped a bit on individual freedom, then so be it. Coming out of the 1960s, moral legitimacy had greater urgency than individual freedom.

———————

IN HIS MEMOIR, *My Grandfather's Son*, Supreme Court Justice Clarence Thomas tells a story that illustrates the new liberalism's principle of dissociation. Justice Thomas is only one man, yet his story is archetypal in the way it illustrates the experience of millions of minorities and even many women.

Clarence Thomas was born into a staggering number of disadvantages. His biological father abandoned him at birth. He was raised by an overwhelmed single mother in the urban poverty of Savannah, Georgia, where he knew "hunger with no prospect of eating and cold with no prospect of warmth." Until his mother finally relinquished Clarence and his younger brother to her own parents for raising when Clarence was nine, his young life had been marked primarily by parental abandonment, near starvation, educational deprivation, and the general chaos, dislocation, and humiliation of deep poverty.

His grandfather, whom he quickly came to call "Daddy," was a man of great character and drive who believed utterly in the redeeming power of hard work. He set the boys to work, monitored their television viewing, disallowed their participation in organized sports (a waste of time), and ferociously insisted on the value of education. (He told them that if they died, he would take their bodies to school for three days just to make sure they weren't faking.) He got them into the local Catholic school because he believed it to be more academically rigorous than the public schools. And despite all he had endured as a black in the South in the first half of the twentieth century, he taught the boys that America was rich in opportunities for blacks if they were willing to work.

This was the milieu of honor, steely pride, and hard work that Clarence Thomas grew up in. It echoed Abraham Lincoln's fabled journey from a humble Springfield, Illinois, log cabin to the White House. As an American boy, Thomas wanted into the better Catholic schools in Savannah, Georgia, not to "integrate" them but to compete with the best and hold his own. And he did.

But then, with his admission to Yale University School of Law—surely the pinnacle of intellectual challenge that he had longed for—he underwent a fall, a sudden loss of innocence. At Yale he discovered that his faith in merit as the way to true equality was naïve and set him up to be the fool. From grade school through college he had succeeded academically "despite his race," as his white teachers patronizingly put it. So when he realized that he was at Yale "because of his race," he was crushed.

Still, he was determined to wield excellence against bigotry, so he took the most rigorous courses on the law-school menu—taxation law, corporate law, bankruptcy, and commercial transactions. He even took a class on taxation from a professor famous for flunking black students, and won the man over. But there remained the larger reality that he could not conquer. Yale University had no interest in Clarence Thomas the *human being*, the young man whose life was animated by the struggle not to be given equality, but to literally earn an irrefutable equality. Yale wanted only the black skin, not the human being within that skin, and certainly not that human being's longing for an unqualified equality.

Clarence Thomas became depressed at Yale and seriously considered transferring to law schools in the South, where his worst threat would be old-fashioned racism—racism, unlike Yale's liberalism, that at least did not ask blacks to be grateful when they were being patronized. But there was no money to pick up his life and transfer to another school, and his wife had become pregnant with their first child. A Yale law degree would be his fate.

And it would not be a good fate. Thomas soon found his Ivy League pedigree to be tainted by affirmative action. He interviewed for jobs with law firms in New York, Washington, and Los Angeles and got nowhere. His interrogators did not believe that he was as good as his own grades indicated. They assumed his presence before them was explained by racial preferences, not by talent. It was as if they were saying the pretense was over: Yale could afford tokenism, but they could not. So here affirmative action undermined the credibility of precisely the kind of person it claimed to be helping. One day, Thomas took a 15-cent price sticker from a package of cigars and stuck it on the frame of his Yale law degree "to remind myself of the mistake I'd made by going to Yale." Today, the degree does not hang in his Supreme Court office, having been permanently consigned to the basement of his Virginia home.

It was finally John Danforth—then the attorney general of Missouri, and later a senator from Missouri, who shepherded Thomas through arguably the most contentious Supreme Court confirmation hearing in American history— who offered Clarence Thomas a job in the Missouri Attorney General's office. But suddenly it was Thomas who had a qualm: he wanted assurance that he would be treated the same as everyone else in the office, no better and no worse. Danforth agreed, and the deal was done.

The new liberalism, rushing madly to engineer The Good that it believed would bolster the legitimacy of the nation, often stepped on the very people it sought to help. There is at least a whisper of doubt over my entire generation of educated blacks—a whisper, frankly, of inferiority. Are we where we are because of merit, or because of jerrybuilt, white guilt concepts like affirmative action and "diversity"? How different, really, is diversity's stigmatization of us as "needy victims" from segregation's stigmatization of us as inferiors? In either case, we are put in service to the white American imagination. In segregation, our inferiority served white supremacy; with "diversity," it gave whites a problem *they* could solve to establish their innocence of racism. In both cases we were a means to a white end.

Think of the maddening double bind here. Some would say, for example, that Clarence Thomas—a well-known critic of affirmative action—was nominated by the GOP to serve on the Supreme Court precisely because he was black. His race (not the man himself) would bring moral authority to the Republican Party's opposition to racial preferences.

So which way to go? If he supports affirmative action, he betrays himself and his belief in the true equality of his own people. If he stands by his integrity as a man and rejects affirmative action, out of faith in the ability of his own people to compete with all others, then he is an Uncle Tom.

This is the new liberalism.

13

Dissociation

AT YALE, CLARENCE THOMAS was not the victim of garden-variety American racism; he was fallout from dissociation, the new liberalism's guiding principle. Dissociation ties the decency of individuals and the legitimacy of institutions and government to a *demonstrable* dissociation from America's past sins—racism, sexism, militarism, environmental indifference, and the like. In this new liberalism, dissociation from America's characterological evil was not simply a means to a better world; it was an end in itself, a gesture that proved the decency of individuals and the legitimacy of institutions. (You could, for example, dissociate from American evil and win decency or legitimacy simply by supporting affirmative action, even if that policy utterly failed to achieve its announced goals.) The point is that

America met the great challenges of the 1960s by inventing a faux human virtue—the idea that a vicarious or merely symbolic dissociation from America's evil past counted as a timeless human virtue like courage or honesty or perseverance, all of which require selflessness and sacrifice.

Dissociation is an artificial virtue because its entire reason for being is to avoid the selflessness, sacrifice, and risk that true virtue inevitably involves. It gives us a road to the decency and legitimacy we want while sparing us the difficulty and struggle of true virtue. Dissociation turns virtue into a mask. It gives us the means to construct a "face of The Good." It counts the mere mouthing of glossy ideas of The Good the same as an honest struggle toward what is actually possible.

For example, how does a people emerging from four centuries of racial oppression actually overcome all the damage done by that oppression and reach a true and self-evident equality with others? Dissociation spares America the need to wrestle with this. It asks us only to identify with public policies contrived around vague effusions of The Good, like multiculturalism, diversity, gender equity, etc.

———————

CLARENCE THOMAS'S WHITE CLASSMATES were privileged by the Ivy League imprimatur of their Yale law degrees.

(One of these classmates callously remarked when Thomas finally got the job in Missouri, a backwater by their lights, that it was a terrible waste of a Yale law degree.) But Thomas was disadvantaged by the same Ivy League imprimatur that privileged them because the entire world, understandably, believed that he was at Yale simply because he was black. It wasn't conceivable that he could be one of the best-educated law-school graduates in the country (and one who had challenged himself with an especially rigorous course load); he was Yale's dissociation from America's old evils.

In his job interviews, he was not seen as a real "Yalie"; rather, he was someone Yale was "hosting" for the sake of its own moral legitimacy. It was as if the word "token" was inscribed in scarlet letters on his forehead. And where could he go to protest this kind of bigotry? Even today—after evolving a unique strict-constructionist jurisprudence that is a consistent point of reference for his fellow justices on the high court—he is diminished in the eyes of the larger public by the peculiar impression that was spawned by racial preferences after the 1960s: that blacks in high places are not there by dint of merit, but for the "optics" of dissociation their presence provided. After all, it is now unthinkable that the Supreme Court would not have at least one black justice—a circumstance that makes a black seat on the Court virtually de jure.

Such was the shame of America after the 1960s that it generated a liberalism grounded in dissociation rather than in principle. This was, and remains, a needy liberalism that insists on flattening as many people as possible to the dimension of their group's grievance against America. And so reduced, such people are primed for rescue by the new liberalism. They become its perfect political constituency. And they make a trade: in exchange for rescue (entitlement programs, group preferences, social programs of all sorts, and "redistributive" government policies and regulations), they will certify that the new liberalism is dissociation itself—and that it is superior to conservatism because it is the only politics that decouples America from its evil past.

WHAT IS THE EFFECT OF ALL THIS? It is profound and it follows a simple sequence. America's great shame in the 1960s made dissociation seem the quickest road back to legitimacy for society, individuals, government, corporations, and all other American institutions. If dissociation was actually not the same thing as The Real Good, or redemption from evil, it counted as such in a post-1960s America desperate for moral authority. It was this desperation that elevated dissociation from a means to an end, made it a complete virtue in its own right, a reflection of high character like honesty or courage. Dissociation was The Good.

This was the pattern of neediness that brought Yale University and Clarence Thomas together. Yale needed Thomas more than he needed Yale. But when you make mere dissociation count as The Good, as Yale did, you are cheating. The true and genuine Good in this case would be to ask a long-subjugated people to overcome the underdevelopment that had been inflicted on them so that they could win their way into the Yales of the world in open and fair competition with all others—a competition that would neither punish nor reward them for their race, ethnicity, or gender.

The true Good would include an incentive to minorities to in fact become equal with all others *by talent and merit*. The true Good would ask minorities to assimilate into modernity even if that felt like self-betrayal, like joining the world that had oppressed them. And it would discourage them from building a group identity singularly focused on protest, tempting as that might be. Instead, all would be focused on their becoming competitive. After all, this was precisely the model of advancement that blacks followed in sports and music to such great success. People often dismiss this success as the exception that proves the rule of discrimination elsewhere. But in fact, blacks ran into all manner of discrimination in sports and music. They simply would not be deterred. Their excellence and merit ultimately prevailed over all else.

Why wouldn't this model work in engineering or medicine or business? One reason is that The Good intervenes in these areas with programs and preferences that dissociate institutions from past evils but also communicate a sense of inferiority to minorities. The new liberalism doesn't worry much about whether young blacks have enough basketball courts to play on, or what the condition of those courts might be. Thus blacks are left to their own devices.

But in those areas like public schools, where there is such pressure for institutions to dissociate from past evil, blacks are rarely left to their own devices. Rather, they are seen as a virtual currency of dissociation, and so they are endlessly and thoughtlessly interfered with. Their history of victimization makes them the responsibility of the society that victimized them, which means that—except for sports and music—they are never left alone to find their own voice.

But the ersatz "virtue" of dissociation allows Yale and all other American institutions—as well as minorities—to avoid the wrenching honesty and hard work that the true Good requires. Dissociation is the proverbial devil atop the shoulder whispering into the ears of the powers that be at Yale: you can win dispensation from the ugly past and legitimize your institution if you will simply rustle up some black and brown faces for your campus. And while you're at it, this devil continues, you might want to ban all military recruiters from campus to dissociate the university from America's military adventurism. You might create black, Hispanic, Asian, and women's studies programs to dissociate from the Eurocentric and patriarchal arrogance of Western civilization. You certainly want to "diversify" the look of the faculty, and it wouldn't hurt to give minority students their own spaces or "houses" on campus where they might alleviate the stress of being on a largely white campus by mingling with their own kind. Dissociation turns The Good into a manipulation of appearances, a sleight of hand by which a cosmetic reform stands in for real reform.

And it works. Yale, like virtually all other American institutions, has relegitimized itself by making a cult of diversity. Today these institutions roll along confident in their legitimacy. Yet, after forty years of diversity initiatives in American universities, blacks still have the lowest grade point averages and the highest dropout rates of any student group in America. All those ugly and damning racial gaps in income levels, illegitimacy rates, academic test scores, unemployment rates, and so on remain unchanged. Diversity is about dissociation and legitimacy for American institutions, not the development of former victims. Clarence Thomas, fiercely committed to his own development and ready to work hard for it, could see even as a law-school student that he was a pawn in someone else's game.

———————

OF THE TWO BROAD POLITICAL IDEOLOGIES—liberalism and conservatism—it was liberalism in the 1960s that seized on dissociation as the fastest way back to legitimacy, and thus to power. And this remains liberalism's great advantage over conservatism—its glib dissociation from the past quickly restores legitimacy to American institutions. Conservatism has no quick dissociative mechanism. It lumbers along struggling with difficult principles—principles that even ask America's former victims to take considerable responsibility for their own advancement. Conservatism doesn't offer dissociation. Thus, in a culture won over by dissociation, conservatism seems to be in association with America's evil past.

14

Relativism and Anti-Americanism

B UT HOW DOES this new liberalism signal its dissociation from the past and make its claim on innocence and power? Certainly there are many ways to give the impression that an institution or an individual, or even a public policy or political party, is innocent of America's evil past. And with dissociation we are always talking about impressions of guilt or innocence. But there are two broad controlling ideas that make this impressionism work: relativism and anti-Americanism. Both are ways to establish an imprint of innocence, and thus to dissociate.

This was fallout from the 1960s verdict of character-ological evil. Among other things, this verdict meant that what was deemed great about America—its special mix of democratic principles and individual rights—was, in reality, neither absolute nor universal.

The problem was that these great principles and rights had become associated with America's evil. But this association was not because the principles were evil in themselves; it was because they had been "relativized," meaning they had been applied *relative* to race, gender, class, and even religion, rather than universally. Conceived for the sole purpose of making freedom universal, they were compromised— literally upon conception—by having to function within a hierarchy of inequality in which property-owning white males were at the pinnacle and blacks (only three-fifths human, according to the US Constitution) were at the bottom. This was the hypocrisy that corrupted our genius for freedom and put us in league with precisely the human impulse to take power through the oppression of others that the American Revolution had challenged. In this sense, "relativizing" was the very essence of American evil. On the one hand, there was the most inspired articulation of human freedom ever rendered, and on the other, the "relativizing" of that freedom so that it was limited by the coarsest of human bigotries—resulting in the denial of freedom to millions.

In the 1960s crisis of authority and legitimacy, the democratic principles and individual rights that had prefigured American greatness were denounced as hypocrisies. They were associated with, not dissociated from, American evil. Thus the dilemma: they were of little value in recovering moral authority and legitimacy. They projected hypocrisy above all else. Those eternal values that enabled people to thrive in freedom—individual initiative, personal responsibility, hard work, commitment to family, the pursuit of excellence, delayed gratification—were suddenly jaundiced, because their payoff was relative to race, gender, ethnicity, and so on. They only fully counted for white people.

My own father lived his entire life in accord with all these values, but his initiative and responsibility were thwarted time and again simply because he was black. (He drove a truck for forty years but could never join the Teamsters Union until two weeks before he retired—a lifetime of substandard wages simply because he was black.) He lived in a world that, while bragging of its devotion to freedom, thwarted his freedom relentlessly. He was marked by his race as someone to be exploited, not liberated. He had little standing as a free man, since full freedom was relative to color.

I remember the family gathered around the TV to watch President John F. Kennedy's inauguration speech, one of the greatest ever. Among many memorable lines, Kennedy said: "Let every nation know, whether it wishes us well or ill, that we shall pay any price, bear any burden, meet any hardship, support any friend, oppose any foe, in order to assure the survival and the success of liberty." It was a powerful statement because it was unequivocal and utterly without relativism.

And yet, early in his presidency, President Kennedy decided that he would go a little slower where civil rights were concerned. His brother Bobby (then the attorney general), in a now famous meeting with James Baldwin, among other black intellectuals and civil rights leaders, openly showed his annoyance at their impatience with the country's slow progress toward full civil rights for blacks. Bobby Kennedy grew angry at being lectured to by blacks—and surely, Baldwin would have been lacerating.

The Kennedys were utterly comfortable living within that peculiar relativism that exempted whites from applying their own fight-to-the-death absolutism around freedom to blacks. Like most white Americans, they had been acculturated to see only a "relativized" black humanity—a malleable and adaptable humanity that was not to be taken as seriously as their own. Therefore, it was very likely unimaginable to them, in the early 1960s, that the cause of civil rights for blacks had come to the same "Give-me-liberty-or-give-me-death" absolutism around freedom that had once driven white Americans to revolution.

The framework of principles and individual rights that ensure freedom, and that actually opened the way to American greatness, had been so relativized by America's tolerance of bigotry and duplicity that the entire framework became tainted with American evil. Yet after the 1960s, America was called upon to reestablish its moral authority and legitimacy. How to do this when the scaffolding of principles and rights that had made America the most prosperous and powerful nation in the world was suddenly associated with America's history of hypocrisy and evil?

This was a terrible yet unacknowledged American tragedy: what was indisputably great about America—our unparalleled embrace of individual freedom—was of little help in restoring the nation's moral authority after the 1960s because it was so compromised by the relativism with which it had been applied. We couldn't simply look out upon the vast discontent of the 1960s and say: all right, we will restore our moral authority by invoking our own genius for freedom. America had betrayed that genius too often, had relativized freedom too much and for too long. You couldn't go into a black neighborhood in any American city and argue that individual initiative and personal responsibility were the best way to exploit freedom now that blacks were finally free. People might nod yes, but there was simply too much bad faith—not to mention lack of experience with full freedom. (Easy to overlook even today the fact that millions of Americans—especially blacks and other people of color—were habituated to living in bad faith with America, habituated to hearing freedom celebrated only to have it denied to them.) There was a vapor of evil hanging over American greatness, over the American genius for freedom, so that when we needed it most, it was not easy to invoke that genius without seeming to also invoke that evil.

———————

THE NEW LIBERALISM that emerged from the 1960s answered this dilemma in a shocking way. Though America's great moral fall in the 1960s was caused by centuries of relativizing the timeless principles of freedom (which were literally conceived to resist such relativism), this new liberalism turned right around and embraced relativism all over again. In fact, it saw relativism as a magic, a new moral activism that would enable America to redeem itself. So the very corruption that led to America's fall in the 1960s would now be used to achieve America's redemption. But there was a difference. The new liberalism claimed that it would not relativize the principles of freedom to accommodate white supremacy, or any other hierarchy of inequality; it would relativize these principles only in the interest of The Good—to restore past victims and to redeem past victimizers.

The great ingenuity of post-1960s liberalism was to restore moral authority to the old corruption of relativism by linking it to The Good.

As recently as the 1950s, a black student, who qualified by merit, could be denied admission to certain American universities simply because he or she was black—because admission by merit (a classic principle of freedom) had been made relative to white supremacy. If you were black, your merit was altogether dismissible in deference to white privilege.

The new liberalism embraced this same relativism (your merit is relative to your race) but claimed it would now support minority development and white redemption rather than white supremacy—The Good rather than evil. So today, a black student can be clearly deficient in academic merit and still be admitted to a university that a white student of comparable merit could never get into. Today this black student's presence on campus dissociates his school from the old relativism of white supremacy. So merit for him is now bundled in with his race's dissociational charisma, its power to irrefutably distance whatever institutions it joins from the taint of America's past evils.

Thus, with this added value of dissociation, he easily passes the bar for admission into precisely those universities that are academically over his head—universities that effectively count his dissociational value to the institution as academic merit. Still these universities claim that their practice of relativism only bends the arch of history toward The Good, and that affirmative action is a good thing in its own right that adds value to the classroom experience for all students. *Their* relativism is "inclusive"; the old relativism of white supremacy was only "exclusionary."

America's interminable debates over affirmative action, diversity, multiculturalism, inclusion, and so on are, in the end, debates over the use of relativism as an instrument of The Good. The many Supreme Court rulings on affirmative action are all rather labored efforts to adjudicate an ongoing American conflict: on the one hand, there is a Constitution written in the faith that its principles will be applied in strict devotion to their original intent; on the other hand, there is a desire to bend those principles to the service of whatever we currently see as The Good. So far, the Court has never completely rejected the latter argument: that a little relativism around those demanding principles is acceptable when it might facilitate The Good by, for example, allowing for race and gender preferences.

What the majority of the Court seems to have missed in all these rulings is that relativism *was* the original sin. This impulse to have the great opportunities of freedom apply relative to everyone's collective identity was always America's fundamental moral corruption. Whether relativism is justified by white supremacy or by diversity, it still privileges some citizens and oppresses others for reasons having nothing to do with who they are as individuals. It always argues for itself in the name of The Good, but for good or ill, it is always antidemocratic, always assigning a preference to some and abusing the freedoms of others.

NEVERTHELESS, THIS RELATIVISM has become the heart and soul of post-1960s liberalism, because it triggers a precise sequence of steps that lead inexorably to raw political power. First, there is the relativism itself—the simple willingness to relativize (and even scorn) the principles and disciplines that made possible the freedom and cultural greatness of Western civilization. Multiculturalism is an example of a liberal idea. It diminishes the singular greatness of the West in relation to other cultures so as to make possible the second step in this sequence: dissociation. If these fine, freedom-nurturing principles are tainted with hypocrisy and evil, then people can honorably—and with even a certain self-congratulation—dissociate from them. And once dissociated, they reach surely not a heaven but definitely a place of innocence, an inner sense of reassurance that they are not that ugly American who brags about "the land of the free" but then easily abides the oppression of others. It is a feeling, above all else, that one is decent and in good faith with the idealism of the American creed: that "all men are created equal."

And, in turn, this sense of innocence easily translates into moral authority and legitimacy—the third step in the formula leading to power. And moral legitimacy, of course, amounts to an entitlement to pursue power. If an individual or a political party is clearly dissociated from the nation's past evils—has displayed a disdain for those evils—then they have achieved a new innocence and are almost obliged to pursue power for the sake of the general good.

This formula—*relativism to dissociation to legitimacy to power*—enables post-1960s liberalism to present itself to the American people not as an ideology or even as a politics, but as nothing less than a moral and cultural imperative. Its raison d'être, its all-informing idea, is that same dark epiphany from the 1960s: that America has evil embedded in its very character. Today's liberalism casts itself as the antidote to that evil, and it asks for a political mandate to bend—or relativize—the principles and values (individual responsibility and initiative, the pursuit of excellence, competition by merit, and so on) that enable people to thrive in freedom in order to make a new society that transcends that evil. If allowed to go unrelativized, the reasoning goes, these principles and values would stand in the way of the social engineering required to fashion a new society. They do not, for example, guarantee a perfect equality or parity between blacks and whites or any other groups in levels of educational achievement, home ownership, wealth acquisition, or any realm of life in which one demographic group can be measured against another. They simply offer no way to throw together the illusion of a society shed of its past.

So this liberalism doesn't want only the middling power to work within the framework of these principles and values—

to only tweak and nudge things here and there toward its ideas of The Good, making sure never to compromise principle. It wants precisely the power and authority to compromise principle, to make these demanding principles relative to The Good. (Better for a corporation to recruit its management out of a commitment to "diversity" than to follow the principle of merit-based hiring.) This liberalism wants the power to *engineer* the transformation of American culture itself away from the evil and hypocrisy it was convicted of in the 1960s and into a new innocence—an innocence that is ecumenical and tolerant, nonhierarchical and nonpatriarchal, and cleansed of all the 1960s charges against the American character.

This is a grand and amorphous vision, perhaps even a little manic. It is a liberalism that doesn't want the hard-earned and unglamorous fairness that struggling with demanding principles would bring. Instead, it chases utopian projections of fairness like "diversity," "gender equity," "sustainability," "social justice," "ecological balance," and "multiculturalism"—vague projections that ring of good intentions for the future at the same time that they admonish America for its past. All these projections are new formulations of innocence meant to answer specific charges of evil from the 1960s.

And these projections are supported by true belief rather than by hard fact–based reason, because their purpose is not to actually achieve anything; it is primarily to offer those who buy into them an identity of innocence, and thus an ongoing entitlement to power. These projections are dissociational, and they comprise a language of identity, a way of broadcasting to the world that one is, as a humble human being, innocent of America's evil past. To embrace any or all of these projections is to scream at the world, "No! I am not of the America that partook of evil. No doubt others are, but not me!"

And wasn't this the essential appeal of Barack Obama's "Hope and Change" campaign? Didn't he essentially put himself forward as a utopian projection, a grand yet amorphous political vision that virtually promised a new age of American innocence—a "post-partisan" and "post-racial" America—without ever making it clear how we would achieve such a society? Didn't Obama tap into a deep American craving for innocence of its past, and didn't that craving transmogrify into his special charisma?

15

The Culture

I WAS RECENTLY INVITED to make some remarks at a charity dinner for a cause that I strongly support. The organizers worried that because their cause only affected Third World nations, they would have a hard time raising money from an American audience. Localism, it seemed, in everything from farm produce to charity giving, was the new vogue. People wanted to see their dollars at work locally rather than watch them disappear into the coffers of some international organization. Could I help them make the case for international giving?

On the night of the dinner it occurred to me to make the point that America was the world's exceptional nation—not that its people were superior, but that its wealth and power bestowed upon it a level of responsibility in the world that

other nations did not have to bear. Exceptionalism as a burden, not a vanity, was my point. Through my wife I had had
an involvement with a charitable organization that focused
on the problem of obstetric fistula in Africa. On a visit to
Africa on behalf of that group, I was pleasantly surprised
to see how much we Americans were respected for our compassion and generosity, quite apart from our wealth and
military power. The people I met saw something essentially
good in the American people. On one blazing hot afternoon
in a remote village in the nation of Niger, a local chieftain,
dramatically bedecked in the head wrap and flowing robe of
his desert people, told me through an interpreter that it was
striking to him to meet people who would come halfway
around the world to help his people—to visit, as he said in
a phrase that mixed pathos with eloquence, "a country lost
in the sun."

I recounted this story at the charity dinner simply to
make the point that American exceptionalism in the world
had as much to do with the largess of our character as with
our great wealth and power, and that causes like the one
at hand only enhanced our reputation in the world as a
fundamentally decent nation—a beacon, as it were, of human possibility. I thought this would be the easiest of points
to make. And things were in fact going smoothly until I
uttered the words "American exceptionalism." Instantly—
almost before I could get the words out of my mouth—quiet

boos erupted from one side of the banquet room. Not loud ugly boos, but polite remonstrative boos, the kind that respectfully censure you for an impropriety. I was shocked. This was a young, bright, prosperous American audience reproaching me for mentioning the exceptionalism of our nation. It was as if they were saying, "Don't you understand that even the phrase American exceptionalism is a hubris that evokes the evils of white supremacy? It is an indecency that we won't be associated with."

In booing, these audience members were acting out an irony: they were good Americans precisely because they were skeptical of American greatness. Their skepticism was a badge of innocence because it dissociated them from America's history of evil. To unreservedly buy into American exceptionalism was, for them, to turn a blind eye on this evil, and they wanted to make the point that they were far too evolved for that. They would never be like those head-in-the-sand Americans who didn't understand that American greatness was tainted by evil. And you could hear—in the spontaneity of their alarm, like a knee jerking at the tap of a rubber hammer—that their innocence of this evil was now a central part of their identity. It was reflex now; they didn't have to think about it anymore.

———————————

IN ITS HUNGER FOR INNOCENCE, post-1960s liberalism fell into a pattern in which anti-Americanism—the impulse, as the cliché puts it, to "blame America first"—guaranteed one's innocence of the American past. Here in anti-Americanism was the Left's all-defining formula: relativism-dissociation-legitimacy-power. Anti-Americanism is essentially a relativism—a false equivalency—that says America, despite her greatness, is no better an example to the world than many other countries. And in this self-effacement there is a perfect dissociation from the American past, and thus a new moral legitimacy—and so, finally, an entitlement to power.

If, at the charity dinner, I had found a way to sneer a little at America, I might have elicited a few cheers from that same side of the room (obviously an in-crowd) that had booed my reference to American exceptionalism. But cheers or boos, that side of the audience only reinforced what most Americans already suspect: that in the culture war between liberalism and conservatism that followed the tumultuous 1960s, liberalism won. That is, liberalism won the moral authority, the power, to set the terms of social relations among Americans—the manners, the protocols, the ideas of decency, the rules for how people must interact within the most diverse society in human history. Liberalism gave America a new "correctness" that enforced these new rules with the threat of stigmatization. There are still, certainly, ferocious debates between liberals and conservatives in many realms—economic policy, education, foreign policy, immigration, the environment, and so on. And these debates will surely grind on.

But post-1960s liberalism won a certain moral hegemony over the culture by establishing *dissociation* as the über human value—the value that literally arbitrates the importance and relevance of all other values. Even those timeless, conventional values that people in earlier times never thought to challenge now come under the purview of dissociation. Could a public official, for example, discuss the weakening of personal responsibility and the work ethic (two timeless values) in some segments of the black community as even a partial cause of the academic achievement gap between blacks and whites in American schools? Of course not. It is simply unthinkable.

The über value of dissociation declares any emphasis on personal responsibility or the work ethic—or any other such self-demanding value—to be racist when used to explain minority weakness. Insistence on values like these seems to put victims in double jeopardy. It makes them the victims of both oppression and their own irresponsibility— implying that their own laziness is as much or more a cause of their inferiority as the fact of their oppression. Dissociation suspends this kind of double jeopardy. Dissociation is a cultural template that tries to make America, and the greater Western world, entirely accountable for its past oppressions and *all* the damage done by them. Therefore the idea that the victims may be accountable in some way for their own ongoing weakness is just impermissible. It violates the assignment of guilt and innocence—who is culpable and who is entitled—that dissociation seeks to enforce.

When we look at American exceptionalism through the lens of dissociation, that exceptionalism is transformed into garden-variety white supremacy. Dissociation sees this exceptionalism as proof of America's characterological evil. It ignores two or three millennia of profound cultural evolution in the West, and it marks up the exceptionalism that results from that evolution to little more than a will to dominate, oppress, and exploit people of color. So in this new and facile liberalism, American exceptionalism and white supremacy become virtually interchangeable. Shift one's angle of vision ever so slightly to the left, and there is white supremacy; ever so slightly to the right, and there is American exceptionalism.

———————

WHEN YOU WIN THE CULTURE, you win the extraordinary power to say what things mean—you get to declare the angle of vision that assigns the "correct" meaning. When I was a boy growing up in segregation, racism was not seen as evil by most whites. It was simply recognition of a natural law: that some races were inferior to others and that people needed and wanted to be with "their own kind." Most whites were quite polite about this—blacks were in their place and it was not proper to humiliate them for their lowly position. Racism was not meant to be menacing; it was only a kind of fatalism, an acceptance of God's will. And so most whites could claim they held no animus toward blacks. Their prejudice, if it was prejudice at all, was perfectly impersonal. It left them free to feel compassion and sometimes even deep affection for those inferiors who cleaned their houses, or served them at table, or suckled their babies. And this was the meaning of things.

The polite booing I elicited by mentioning American exceptionalism at the charity dinner also reflected—for the actual booers and their cohorts—simply the meaning of things. It was a culturally conditioned response. American exceptionalism was a scandal that one booed in the name of humility and decency. Dissociation from it was the road to The Good. And this was so sealed a matter that booing me was only an expression of one's moral self-esteem—the goodness in oneself bursting forth to censure a heretic.

16

Conservatism

The New Counterculture

B UT THERE IS MORE TO THE STORY. After the polite boos from one side of the banquet room, there came a round of defiant cheers from the other side of the room— as if the booers and the cheerers had staked out their own territories. Clearly the cheers were a challenge to the idea that American exceptionalism was somehow anathema, something to be booed. I appreciated the moral support, but I knew the cheers had very little to do with me. The tension in the room was between those embarrassed by American exceptionalism and those who took pride in it.

So there it was, within the space of mere seconds, the specter of two very different Americas clashing over a single phrase: American exceptionalism. Post-1960s liberalism had won the culture. The cultural confidence that liberals felt in this explains why they were the first to show their hand by booing—they just presumed that everyone (or at least every decent American) would be happy to boo American exceptionalism. And if people were too shy to actually boo, they would be happy to hear others boo. After all, the new liberalism orbited around the idea that this exceptionalism was the fruit of American evil. This was the established meaning of things. And they were no doubt shocked to hear their boos answered with a wave of polite cheers from the other side of the room. In other words, they were shocked to see that there was another America represented in the room, one that was not so reflexively anti-American. American liberals often think of themselves as a moral vanguard, as the last word in "social justice," yet here was a vigorous counterpoint. What to make of people who actually cheer at the mention of American exceptionalism?

Well, post-1960s liberalism had *so* won over the culture, and become *so* congealed into the new moral establishment, that conservatism—as a politics and philosophy—became a centerpiece in liberalism's iconography of evil. It was demonized and stigmatized as an ideology born of nostalgia for America's past evils—inequality, oppression, exploitation, warmongering, bigotry, repression, and all the rest. Liberalism had won the authority to tell us what things meant and to hold us accountable to those meanings. Conservatism—liberals believed—*facilitated* America's moral hypocrisy. Its high-flown constitutional principles only covered up the low motivations that actually drove the country: the self-absorbed pursuit of wealth, the insatiable quest for hegemony in the world, the unacknowledged longing for hierarchy, the repression of women, the exploitation of minorities, and so on.

Conservatism took the hit for all the hypocrisies that came to light in the 1960s. And it remains today an ideology branded with America's shames. Liberalism, on the other hand, won for its followers a veil of innocence. And this is the gift that recommends it despite its legacy of failed, even destructive, public policies. We can mark up the black underclass, the near disintegration of the black family, and the general decline of public education—among many other things—to liberal social policies. Welfare policies beginning in the 1970s incentivized black women *not* to marry when they became pregnant, thereby undermining the black family and generating a black underclass. The public schools in many inner cities became more and more dysfunctional as various laws and court cases hampered the ability of school officials and classroom teachers to enforce discipline. Meanwhile, the schools fell under the sway of multiculturalism as well as powerful teachers unions that often oppose accountability reforms. Students in these schools, after the welfare-inspired breakdown of the black family, were less and less prepared to learn. Affirmative action presumed black inferiority to be a given, so that racial preferences actually locked blacks into low self-esteem and hence low standards of academic achievement. "Yes, we are weak and noncompetitive and look to be preferred for this; our weakness is our talent." School busing for integration only led to a more extensive tracking system within the integrated schools so that blacks were effectively segregated all over again in the lower academic tracks. And so on. Post-1960s liberalism—on the hunt for white American innocence—has done little more than toy with blacks.

Yet it is conservatives who now feel evicted from their culture, who are made to feel like outsiders even as they are accused of being traditionalists. And contemporary conservatism is now animated by a sense of grievance, by the feeling that the great principles it celebrates are now dismissible as mere hypocrisies.

There is now a new phrase: "movement conservative." When I first heard it, I thought it oxymoronic. Conservatism is establishment and tradition, not protest and reform. But "movement" suggests struggle against injustice, the overcoming of some oppression. So it is telling that many conservatives now think of themselves as part of a "movement," and refer to each other as "movement conservatives." A great irony that slowly emerged out of the turmoil of the 1960s is that conservatism became the new counterculture—a movement that was subversive in relation to the established liberal cultural order. And, continuing this irony, liberalism became the natural home of timid conventionalists and careerists—people who find it hard to know themselves outside the orthodoxies of mainstream "correctness." And what is political correctness if not an establishment orthodoxy?

What drives this new conservative "movement"? Of course there are the classic motivations—a faith in free-market capitalism, smaller government, higher educational standards, the reinforcement of family life, either the projection of strength abroad or, conversely, a kind of isolationism, and so on. But overriding all of this is a cultural motivation that might be called the "pinch of stigma." The special energy of contemporary conservatism—what gives it the dynamism of a movement—comes from conservative outrage at being stigmatized in the culture as the politics in which all of America's past evils now find a comfortable home.

This stigmatization is conservatism's great liability in an American culture that gives dissociation preeminence, that makes it the arbiter of all other social values. Contemporary conservatism is, first of all, at war with this cultural stigmatization. Its ideas always swim upstream against the perception that they only echo the racist, sexist, and parochial America of old—as if conservatism were an ideology devoted to human regression. For conservatives, it is, in the end, a bewildering war against an undeserved bad reputation. And how do you fight a bad reputation that always precedes you?

This connection of conservatism to America's hypocritical past is the American Left's greatest source of authority. However trenchant conservatism may be on the issues, however time-tested and profound its principles, this liberalism always works to smother conservatism's insights with the poetic truth that conservatism is mere cover for America's characterological evil. This ability to taint conservatism—its principles, policies, and personalities—with America's past shames has been, for the Left, a seemingly endless font of power.

17

A Politics of Idealism

I WAS BORN INTO A FAMILY CONCEIVED IN IDEALISM. Our family would never have existed were it not for the idealisms of racial integration and equality. The lives of my parents—an interracial couple that lived on the black side of America's wall of segregation until they reached the brink of their old age—were animated by idealism. I marched with my parents not only for civil rights but also for world peace. In the 1950s, there was a forty-mile "peace march" every spring from the Great Lakes naval base north of Chicago to a protest rally against nuclear weapons at the famous Chicago Water Tower on North Michigan Avenue near downtown. My mother would offer me up as a marcher every year. Her only lenience, since I was still preteen, was to send me into the march for only the last twenty miles. After twelve or so grueling miles—in a gesture of Gandhian self-flagellation—we always spent the night before reaching downtown in a homeless shelter that invariably reeked of urine, Thunderbird wine, and disinfectant. The idea was to learn compassion—on the way to banning nuclear weapons. I never resisted much. My mother, I knew, was only steeling me for the rigors of idealism.

And the idealism we pursued was premised on the faith that America—and possibly only America—was a great enough nation to realistically pursue things like racial integration and nuclear disarmament. It was an idealism that grew out of a faith in the timeless principles articulated in the Declaration of Independence and the US Constitution (all the betrayals of these principles notwithstanding). My parents, and their like-minded friends, did not assume that the majestic vision of human freedom promised in America's founding documents was a given. Rather, they saw it as an American potential that would have to be fought for and earned. It was the responsibility of good modern Americans to broaden freedom beyond anything Thomas Jefferson or James Madison could have imagined. So they thought of themselves as people in a kind of vanguard of freedom.

The point is that their idealism was based on identification *with*, not against, America. It was an outgrowth of the American creed. They believed that it was precisely social convulsions like the civil rights movement that expanded freedom. My parents married in Chicago in 1944, in violation of existing law in several other states, and against the better judgment of even some of their close friends, who worried for them. But they had internalized their idealism. Their point, as an interracial couple, was that they were not making a point. They were free Americans, and that was the end of it. Researchers investigating interracial marriage would occasionally appear at our front door asking for a "sociological" interview only to have my mother smile politely as she—a stickler for good manners—discreetly closed the door on them. We were not to be "studied."

THIS WAS ALSO THE IDEALISM of the civil rights movement as it developed through the 1950s and into the 1960s. One of the movement's most common signs at protests read simply: "I Am a Man." Martin Luther King's "I Have a Dream" speech was a call to focus on "the content of our character" as the true measure of man. The goal of this movement was to have blacks *join* the society on an equal footing with all other Americans. So King was a reformer rather than a revolutionary—and the leader of arguably America's greatest reform movement ever. He sought to petition the government, not overthrow it. And his point was a simple one:

that race should never abridge the constitutional rights of
any American citizen. Always it was this idea of individual
freedom—as expressed in the Constitution—that provided the political and legal framework for his humanistic
idealism.

But then came what I have called America's great Fall.
As the catalog of American hypocrisies became longer, more
vivid, and more indisputable in the 1960s, America fell from
its rather blind faith in its own innocence into the knowledge that it was distinctly *not* innocent. The archetypal fall
is always a descent from illusion into reality—in this case
from a self-flattering, if forced, sense of innocence into the
reality that America had shaken hands with the devil.

Does this mean that America was not also a great nation?
Certainly not. But it did mean that even its extraordinary
greatness—its unmatched capacity for innovation and pro-
ductivity, its creed of freedom—was not enough to keep
it from shaking the devil's hand. Within its greatness the
all-too-familiar fallibilities of human nature—racism, sexism, militarism, greed, and so on—found ways to manifest
themselves. Thus the charge of characterological evil.

And the almost instantaneous reaction to this Fall was
the emergence of a left/liberal counterculture that sought
to give America a new idealism—not the freedom-based
idealism that I had grown up with, but an idealism of governmental activism that would impose The Good on the

country. The old idealism of freedom was stained with The Fall itself.

In the mid- and late 1960s, I changed horses, as it were, from an idealism of individual freedom and equality of opportunity (every white man's birthright) to a new idealism in which governmental activism—in the name of some Good like "integration" or "environmental protection"—would try to literally manufacture a desired result. Minorities would be shoehorned into equality with racial preferences. Public schools would be school-bused into integration. Endangered species would live in "protected habitats." And all this only seemed reasonable, given America's fallen state.

It was exactly this insight—that America was fallen and therefore vulnerable to guilt about its past—that gave me a sense of entitlement. Suddenly I was not just owed the same level of freedom that whites enjoyed; I was owed the same life that whites enjoyed. And if there was any disparity between my life and theirs—in income or educational achievement or wealth accumulation—then that was proof of ongoing discrimination. "Disparate impact" became the new measure of injustice. The government was called upon to socially engineer us past such disparities— to come up with policies and programs that would take us from a disparity of results to an equality of results.

It was an inevitable sequence: society's brave acknowledgment of past wrongs fueled a sense of entitlement within

minorities that could only be assuaged through governmental activism. This was the new idealism that seduced me in
the late 1960s. The logic seemed so clear: now that the over-
whelming wrong done to blacks had been acknowledged,
the smart thing for us as blacks was to change the very
goal of our protest against America from the achievement
of freedom to the establishment of our entitlement. Our
identity as a people who had taken charge of their own fate,
and honorably fought for and won freedom against all odds,
against even an often indifferent government, would give
way to an identity grounded in aggrievement, on the one
hand, and entitlement, on the other. This logic—coming
out of the perception that whites were at last ashamed of
America's racist past—suddenly became the most powerful
leverage American minorities had ever known. In fact, white
guilt over the past was literally the measure of minority
leverage. Freedom was good, but now we had the leverage
to demand an actual equality of results. Even as a college
student I felt the power of this idea.

But there was a catch. The leverage we gained by rely-
ing on America's sense of fallenness came at the price of
taking on, and then living with, an identity of grievance
and entitlement. I did not understand at the time that this
was a fool's bargain, a formula for self-defeat—that it drew
minorities into a Faustian pact by which we put our fate in
the hands of contrite white people. Very often they were

honorable people who simply found it hard to live with history's accusation that they were racist, people who wanted to shout: "Other whites, yes, but not me."

The problem was that, in taking this route, we relinquished considerable control over our own destiny. Rather than seizing as much control over our fate as possible after our civil rights victories of the 1960s, we turned around and looked to the government for the grand schemes that would result in our uplift. It was the first truly profound strategic mistake we made in our long struggle for complete equality. It made us a "contingent people" whose fate depended on what others did for us. Thus it relegated us to the sidelines of our own aspirations. It left us pleading with the government, not for freedom, which we had already won, but for "programs" and "preferences" that would be a ladder to full equality. The chilling result is that now, fifty years later, we remain—by most important measures—in the position of inferiors and dependents.

However, even as I first embraced this new idealism/liberalism, I felt its paternalism to be far more maddening and smothering than anything I had known in full-out segregation. At least after the countless rejections I had endured growing up in segregation, there was no (or very little) psychological enmeshment with my oppressors. They didn't expect me to show gratitude, and certainly didn't concern themselves with what I thought or felt about them.

Whites found their superiority in disregarding the humanity of blacks altogether. And, paradoxically, the absoluteness of this disregard left blacks to their own resources and to the possibility of a defiant, even profound, dignity. We would find ways to assert the fullness of our humanity no matter society's dismissal of us. With the new post-1960s idealism/liberalism, our humanity was not demeaned; it was simply beside the point. In this liberalism, we were more important as symbols and tokens of white innocence than as human beings.

I REMEMBER THAT IN THE EARLY 1970S in graduate school, there was a white male student who made a point of being my friend. I didn't understand why, because we had very little in common. I was open to friendship, but nothing he talked about interested me much; likewise, he seemed indifferent to much of what I wanted to talk about. Then something disturbing happened. In a crowd of fellow graduate students, all white but for me, he told what can only be described as a stupid racist joke—something coming out of the antiquated imagery of the minstrel tradition of blackface, watermelons, and cotton picking. (Amazing the durability of this imagery.) Then he looked at me, as if to say my black friend here will laugh along with us, and thus confirm that we are innocent of real racial animus, precisely because we can laugh at such a joke in his presence. His presence makes absurd the idea that we are racists.

I was a pawn in the drama of his innocence. He wasn't interested in staking out his right to be a racist. Quite the opposite: he was telling a racist joke for no other reason than to assert his innocence of racism. And my role was to vet him as an innocent.

This is the dynamic of the new liberalism. Superficially, it is very "caring" toward blacks, minorities, and the poor. It befriends them, promises them all manner of programs and policies. It makes a show of being deferential toward their woundedness, of bowing before their past victimization as before an irrefutable moral authority. But, of course, all this deference is a seduction. The new liberalism does not pursue the actual uplift of minorities and the poor. It pursues dispensation from America's past sins for whites—the imprimatur of innocence. Minorities and the poor, seduced by all the promises scattered like rose petals in their path, are thus manipulated into bestowing that imprimatur.

This was the manipulation that my fellow graduate student worked on me when he told his racist joke in front of other whites, and then pulled for me to laugh at it. Because he didn't really know me, he didn't understand how deeply ingrained my racial pride was. It was not a fashionable politics or an intellectual position; it was an atavistic and involuntary reflex. I would not endure even the slightest transgression of black dignity—that is to say, any hint of white supremacy.

So I saw everything in a flash. He was going to laugh at blacks and then congratulate himself for doing so. He was going to dredge up odious black stereotypes precisely to signal his innocence of them. My role was to laugh along with him and thus confirm his absence of malice. He would be a fellow hail-and-well-met living a new kind of white life in which joining the new idealism/liberalism granted him an identity of innocence where race was concerned—and therefore immunity from all charges of racism. Thus, secure in his innocence, he could tell a racist joke as a kind of braggadocio, as a way of showing off his immunity. He could snatch a laugh off of the oppression that white America had inflicted on my people, and then solicit a conspiratorial laugh from me.

There is always a point at which enough becomes enough. And here the level of my anger scared me. It was more existential than personal. There is a callowness in human nature out of which evil flows blithely. So it wasn't just the racial insult that fueled my anger; it was also the fatigue at once again seeing this feature of the human character so nakedly—at seeing yet again, as a black, that I might always be up against some smallness, some moral blindness, endemic to the human condition. It injured my hopefulness and filled me with as much sadness as rage. I wanted to hit him, but what would it have meant?

I settled for walking away from him. But the rage remained, and as I ran into situations like this again and again, it deepened as the years passed. As the new liberalism unfolded in the decades after the 1960s, it became clear to me that liberalism was pulling for congratulation from blacks in the same way that my fellow graduate student had pulled for me to laugh at his racist joke. This liberalism was a political and ideological framework that asked me to do the same thing he had asked me to do: to reward even the slightest misguided gesture or expression of white goodwill with immunity from any association with America's ugly past. Immunity was the first and greatest goal of this liberalism, never the development of minorities.

Were liberals like my fellow graduate student cynically duplicitous or simply deluded? I could never see much difference.

SO FOR MINORITIES, the bargain such liberals offered was a terrible trap. It required minorities to see white goodwill as the great transformative force that would lift them into the full equality they could never reach on their own. It enmeshed their longings for equality with white longings for redemption. Through this liberalism, the government took a kind of benevolent dominion over the fate of minorities and the poor, not to genuinely help them (which would require asking from them the hard work and sacrifice that real development requires), but to achieve immunity for the government from the taint of the past.

If I had laughed at my fellow graduate student's joke, I would have vetted his innocence of America's past evils. Post-1960s liberalism pulls for the same vetting. It wants minorities to accept their own inferiority so that they might be delivered from it by government interventions driven by the nation's remorse over the past.

The tragedy here is that this liberalism asks minorities to believe that the inferiority imposed on them is their best leverage in society—thus making inferiority the wellspring of their entitlement and power even as it undermines the incentive to overcome it. This is the dynamic that causes post-1960s liberalism to mimic precisely the same hierarchical patterns that the ideology of white supremacy imposed—whites as superiors; minorities as inferiors who must be redeemed through the agency of others.

BY THE MID- TO LATE 1970s I had begun, almost surreptitiously, to hear other voices and to listen to other ideas. I knew very clearly that I still stood for that freedom-focused idealism I had grown up with, the idealism that had animated the original civil rights movement. I still wanted the same things from my society—not special or preferential treatment, not big interventionist programs that would presume to engineer me into equality; just equality under the law, and the unequivocal right to pursue the American dream as I saw fit within the law.

Increasingly—and to my great surprise—I found the idealism I believed in more in what conservatives were saying than in what liberals said. Conservatives didn't want to take you over, make you a pawn in some abstract policy goal, like "integration" or "diversity." They wanted to apply the discipline of freedom to problems of race and poverty, and even to the problems of the great middle class. They understood that freedom was equal opportunity in itself. What had to end were the evils of persecution and discrimination, the eternal enemies of freedom. After these enemies were pushed back (and this came to pass), it was up to minorities to fully find their way into the modern world.

No doubt, remnants of the old evils would remain, but they would not be enough to dissuade minorities of their aspirations. I found conservatism, unlike liberalism, to offer the stark fairness of true freedom in which both success and failure are always possible, a fairness of disinterested equanimity. In this kind of fairness there was respect for minorities as people who could be competitive with all others once they were spared persecution and discrimination. Surely it would take some time to make up for the deficits that centuries of oppression had caused, but only the impartiality of true freedom—uncontaminated by group preferences and governmental paternalism—would provide exactly the right incentives to do precisely this.

Government interventions only shield people from necessity, hold out the false promise of safe harbor, and inadvertently give the impression that a good argument for entitlement (because of past victimization) can bring the same results as hard work, an uncompromising commitment to education, and a spirit of self-help—values that actually enable people to prosper in freedom. Plain, disinterested freedom clarifies all of this. So yes, conservatism offers minorities a starker freedom than liberalism does—a "flat freedom," like a flat tax that treats everyone exactly the same. But this is a good thing, because it reinforces the values that minorities will most need in freedom. It puts their fate back into their own hands and spares them the illusion of deliverance by others.

And yet post-1960s liberalism had won the culture. Faith in governmental intervention had become the conventional wisdom. But the very hegemony of this liberalism triggered blowback; in response to it, conservatism underwent a revival. By winning the culture, liberalism had forced conservatism into the role of a "counterculture," a resistance movement, as it were, comprised of people who found themselves labeled "outsiders" precisely because of their faith in the principles that defined the American democracy. Like the liberals of the 1950s and 1960s, who also felt themselves to be "outsiders" protesting an establishment, conservatives suddenly saw that they needed to contest liberalism's capture of the political and cultural establishment.

Slowly, conservatism accepted that it would have to function essentially as a reformist movement. In other words, conservatism—for all its grounding in timeless democratic principles, and its willingness to be informed by the wisdom of tradition—would have to function more as an activism. It could no longer be content to simply recite the great principles of democracy and freedom; it would have to become an ideology in its own right—an ideology in contention with liberalism. Conservatism would have to take on the passion of idealism. Part of Ronald Reagan's genius was that he embraced his conservatism with great passion out of his conviction that it would make a better world. In him conservatism found a new synthesis of two often opposing elements of political life: the moral rigor of demanding principles, on the one hand, and the passion and charisma of idealism, on the other.

Ronald Reagan practiced conservatism as a transformative faith. He did not run for the presidency as a "sane moderate," or as a managerial type who would only strive to keep the ship of state on an even keel. He wanted to take America to a new and better place than he thought liberalism ever could. This is why his conservatism rose to the level of an idealism. It captured the imagination of even those working-class "Reagan Democrats" who normally felt little attraction to Republicans. When people listened to him, they heard a fatherly resoluteness of principle so utterly self-assured that it could speak to all Americans with forbearance, kindness, and even humor.

———————

I NEVER VOTED FOR RONALD REAGAN. I would catch myself listening to him, and even admiring him, but I could not bring myself to actually vote for him. The conditioning of my background as a black born into a segregated world was simply insurmountable. It was not until the middle of his second term in office that I was hit with a series of epiphanies that opened me to Ronald Reagan. I had come to feel exhausted with and humiliated by liberalism, which seemed to be premised on the idea of permanent black inferiority—on the idea that blacks would always need special programs and preferences to reach anything like true equality.

In my revulsion at this form of liberalism, it occurred to me that Ronald Reagan was something of a liberator. He aspired to what I came to think of as "flat freedom," in which everyone was treated the same and required to live by the same laws. No guilt over the past, no paternalism, no longing for redemption should interrupt the "flatness" of this freedom. Like the flat tax, in which everyone pays the same tax rate, flat freedom makes no exceptions, offers no deductions for past injustices, and gives no preferences to engineer "social justice." Reagan was inviting blacks to function as free men and women in a free society.

The implication of this was that he truly believed that blacks and other minorities were in fact equal to white Americans, and that in a society committed to flat freedom, they could compete with all others. Liberalism was wobbly on this matter; its policies always compensated for the possibility of real black inferiority. Reagan's conservatism— his idealism—was based on a conviction that blacks were fundamentally equal to all other races.

Conservatism became my new idealism. Here was true and unencumbered freedom—the absence of both discrimination and patronizing interference.

18

Liberalism Is Beautiful, but Conservatism Is Freedom

BACK IN THE 1960s, William F. Buckley began to host *Firing Line* on public television, one of the best public affairs talk shows ever. For decades, there he would be every week—fidgeting with a pencil or pen, a clipboard balanced precariously on his knee, his clothes slightly rumpled— interrogating his guests in a high-toned, prep-school accent so utterly pretentious that it was a parody of itself. It was all part of his shtick, along with eyebrows that seemed to leap up in alarm over rapidly blinking eyes. His ticks caricatured him, became a part of his legend.

In college I watched him adversarially. Back then I lived on the borderline between liberalism and radicalism, and I watched him out of a morbid curiosity. I watched precisely to root against him. Yet I liked him because he seemed fearless. He clearly thrived on intellectual challenge, and his encounters with his staunchest opponents only brought out the best in him. Still, I felt a little sorry for him when he announced that he would soon debate James Baldwin at Cambridge University on the subject of race in America.

While Buckley was a dazzling writer and debater, Baldwin—steeped in the moralism of Charles Dickens and the rhetorical richness of the King James Bible—was even more dazzling at both. I had read everything he'd written—several of his essays many times over—and I had seen him literally wither his opposition on several talk shows. I thought Buckley, Yale pedigree and all, was finally in for a thrashing.

I couldn't have been more wrong. Buckley scalpeled his way through Baldwin's arguments with utter aplomb, with sharp, reasoned challenges based on the constitutional tenets of freedom—on the first principles of the Bill of Rights to which both men, as born and bred Americans, subscribed. Baldwin looked overwhelmed, as flat as unleavened bread. I had waited for this encounter the way one waits for a heavyweight title fight only to have my fighter hit the canvas in the early rounds. I was deflated. Worse, I saw for the first time that Baldwin's arguments were too much based on his outrage and indignation at racial injustice. The easy appeal of his outrage in a society newly contrite over its racial history had spoiled him a bit. Buckley was not dismissive of this outrage; he simply proceeded as if it were interesting but not really relevant.

And yet, if Baldwin lost the debate for his overreliance on outrage, Buckley was unable to win it because of his overreliance on principle and reason.

Buckley could not win—although he had defeated his opponent by logic—because he failed to fully appreciate one thing: the *bad faith* that four centuries of oppression inevitably breeds into the life and culture and psychology of a long-oppressed people. So Buckley, for all his brilliance at wielding the principles of freedom, was finally only fluent where he no doubt wanted to be profound. He missed the larger story: that for those oppressed by America's hypocrisy and evil, disbelief and bad faith had become a kind of collective wisdom—a knowledge within the group, even a theme of the group identity. The group prided itself in its skepticism toward the very principles of freedom that Buckley celebrated. The slightest stretch of imagination should have led Buckley to at least vaguely understand this: How could people who had been debased and dehumanized for centuries—and who were still in the throes of fighting for their full freedom and dignity—have unreserved good faith in the US Constitution and all its wonderful principles?

Precisely because America is a society founded on such high principles, its indulgence in racism pushes the victims of racism onto an existential plane where good faith—a trust that the world essentially means what it says ("all men are created equal")—becomes a farce. In other words, oppression dispirits its victims by making them the butt of a cosmic joke: believe and strive all you want, but you will get nowhere. It's the old Malcolm X line: Question—"What is a black man with a PhD?" Answer—"A nigger."

Bad faith is a cultural habit of disbelief and suspicion toward the society in which one lives. Most Americans have a healthy skepticism toward their government. But the bad faith that follows from having suffered real oppression in one's own society requires an almost blanket skepticism toward that society as a survival mechanism. Accept that your society is always lying to you so as to exploit you. Start from this reality; make it the premise of all else you think about your society.

Even though Baldwin's performance in that interview was without his usual dazzle and insight, he was the more profound of the two. Buckley was sharp and crisp, brilliant as always, but he lacked imagination—specifically, the empathetic imagination to see his way into another man's experience, to simply imagine what it must be like to come from the other man's world. So he won the debate but lost it too. And so it may well be that Baldwin lost and yet won.

THE AMERICAN LEFT went in Baldwin's direction after the 1960s. Something sweeping and restorative seemed called for, something big enough to make a high drama of America redeeming herself from her own hypocrisies and evils. This was a far more urgent mandate than Buckley's stern discipline of principles. When I stumbled upon his TV show in the 1970s, he was still compelling, but he seemed to me a study in irrelevance. There was no pressing call in the culture for his views. Even Richard Nixon and Gerald Ford were liberals by his standards. So he was, in that era, a quixotic figure. Baldwin was the culture, the new establishment.

Yet, as the Left mounted one grand scheme after another, it also launched itself into a long arc of utter failure. The War on Poverty, busing for integration, welfare without the requirement of even the most fundamental of human responsibilities, the spoils system of affirmative action, the ongoing corruption and silliness of "diversity," with its diminution of Americans into their mere demographic categories—race, gender, ethnicity, and sexual orientation—all this and more is failure writ large for the American Left. This kind of Balkanization only dehumanizes in the name of humanizing.

The genius of the Left was to unveil the tragedy of American hypocrisy and evil. The Left's downfall will be its overreaching efforts to redeem the nation of those evils. The Left will fail as long as it keeps trying to fashion an ideology in reaction to America's past sins.

I believe today's political Right has the best roadmap to the future—free markets, free individuals in a free society, and the time-tested apparatus of principles and values that make freedom possible. Perhaps Mr. Buckley's time has come. But the merits of the Right's ideas will not be enough to bring them into realization. The Right will have to subsume some of the Left's territory—that is, it will have to give clear and heartfelt witness to the struggles of the middle and working classes and to the alienation and bad faith of those groups that have suffered America's hypocrisy for generations. This is not to say that they should compromise principle— the Left tried this and utterly failed. But the Right must look frankly at the needs of the middle and working classes and at the psychological and cultural damage done to mi- norities by American hypocrisy, and show how its ideas can constitute a redemption—an American dream truly open to everyone.

The point is that redemption is necessary. The principles of freedom themselves must be redeemed. The Left succeeds despite its record of failure because it seized dominion over this redemption, pitched its moral activism as the means to its realization. The Right struggles more than it should because it has failed to show how principles—rather than "moral" activism—are America's *only* defense against hypocrisy. After all, these are the principles that finally brought the civil rights movement its great victories. But the Right has been flummoxed by the Left's power to stigmatize it with America's infamous past hypocrisies. In the culture, the Left has made the Right into a stand-in for America's past evils. And it is hard to fight against a cultural perception so entrenched as to be conventional wisdom.

The Right will have to compete for the culture—to work even harder on the cultural level than it does on the political level. The Left has made government intervention the redemption from old America and the road to a new and better America. And this is the Right's opportunity, because the government is guaranteed failure. Here is the opportunity for the Right to make a point more deeply grounded in the human experience: it is only the *initiative* of human beings—individually and collectively—that can redeem a people from a trying past and deliver them to a better future. Only human initiative is transformative, and it is an eternal arrogance of the Left to assume that government can somehow engineer or inspire or manipulate transformation. You cannot help people who have not already taken initiative—meaning *total* responsibility for their future. And it takes very little to help those who have actually taken such responsibility.

It will never be different than this.

The victim of oppression is always, and understandably, startled and resentful of the anxieties and burdens that new freedom entails—its call to greater responsibility, discipline, and sacrifice. But there it is.

When Buckley debated Baldwin, a broad expanse of national guilt lay between them—a territory that we Americans have been negotiating now for centuries. And in the light of history I think it will be seen as a valiant negotiation—wrenching, often stupid, always informative, and somehow inspiring to us all. I believe that it has deepened and expanded the American character. No nation has struggled harder to overcome the barriers to our common humanity, or to sanctify the individual, than America. The contortions of our hyperbolic politics can be depressing. But America's essential truth—the deepest theme of our identity—is still freedom. Freedom is still our mother tongue.